HYPERINFLATION HAVOC

Hyperinflation Havoc

Limits on Government Printing

SANYUB S.

Spectra Enterprise

Contents

INDEX

Chapter 7: Navigating the Future
7.1 Implementing Sustainable Economic Policies
7.2 Global Cooperation in Monetary Stewardship
7.3 Lessons Learned and Strategies for a Stable Financial Future

INTRODUCTION

Hyperinflation is a phenomenon that occurs in the economy and is defined by inflation that is of an extraordinarily high level and typically increases. The real value of a nation's currency is rapidly depreciated as a result of this, which ultimately results in a loss of faith in the monetary system. An excessive amount of money being printed by the government is one of the key factors that contribute to hyperinflation. It is possible for governments to resort to printing money in order to meet their short-term financial needs; nevertheless, when this practice is carried out without any restraint, it has serious consequences. The causes and effects of hyperinflation, as well as the historical cases in which it occurred, are discussed in this article. Additionally, the constraints that the government should place on printing in order to prevent such economic calamities are also discussed.

Things that lead to hyperinflation:

A Rapid Increase in the Money Supply: Hyperinflation is sometimes caused by a rapid increase in the money supply that outpaces the expansion of commodities and services in the economy. The market is flooded with money when governments print an excessive amount of it, which results in an imbalance between the quantity of money and the amount of products and services that are available.

Mismanagement of the fiscal system: Poor fiscal policies, such as significant budget deficits and spending by the government that cannot be sustained, are components that contribute to hyperinflation. When governments are confronted with budget deficits, they may turn to printing money in order to finance their spending, which can lead to a spiral of inflation through the economy.

In many cases, hyperinflation is followed by a loss of confidence in the national currency. This is because hyperinflation inflates prices quickly. People are trying to spend their money as quickly as possible because they are anticipating additional devaluation, which is making the inflationary pressures even worse.

Ineffectiveness of Monetary Policy Central banks play an essential part in the process of managing inflation through the use of monetary policy. On the other hand, a government can be a contributor to hyperinflation if it interferes with the independence of the central bank or if it implements monetary policies that are ineffective.

Exemplifications of Hyperinflation Throughout History:

After the end of World War I, the Weimar Republic in Germany experienced what is considered to be the most notorious instance of hyperinflation. This occurred during the years 1921-1923. In order to satisfy the war reparations, the German government resorted to printing a large amount of money, which resulted in hyperinflation and left the currency almost completely useless.

In the latter part of the 2000s, Zimbabwe was hit by hyperinflation that reached astronomical heights. This occurred during the years 2007 and 2009. The issuance of trillion-dollar notes, which highlights the destructive impact of unregulated government printing, was caused by a combination of factors, including economic mismanagement, political instability, and land reforms.

Venezuela (2016-2021): Venezuela was confronted with hyperinflation as a result of a confluence of causes, which included economic incompetence, corruption, and the drop of oil prices. As a result of the government's reliance on printing money to meet budget gaps, hyperinflation occurred, which eventually led to the population being impoverished.

The following are the consequences of hyperinflation:

Hyperinflation causes turmoil in the economy because it causes people to lose faith in the currency, which in turn disrupts economic activities. The market is in a state of confusion as a result of the fact that businesses have a difficult time determining pricing and customers rush to spend their money before its worth increases even further.

Erosion of Wealth: The real value of savings and investments is eroded by hyperinflation, which results in the destruction of wealth for both individuals and businesses. People frequently turn to alternate stores of value, such as foreign currencies or tangible assets, which contributes to the devaluation of the currency.

Discontentment in Society The economic upheaval that is brought on by hyperinflation can bring about social discontentment as well as political instability. It is possible that under extreme circumstances, it will lead to demonstrations, strikes, and a breakdown of social order as individuals fight to achieve their fundamental requirements.

International Implications The hyperinflation that occurs in one nation can have global repercussions, particularly in a world that is more interconnected. The disruption of financial markets, the disruption of trade links, and the creation of uncertainty for international investors are all potential outcomes.

Printing restrictions imposed by the government:

Independent Central Banks It is essential to establish and preserve the independence of central banks in order to significantly reduce the amount of intervention that the government has in monetary policy. A central bank that is independent is able to make judgments that are based on the fundamentals of the economy rather than on political concerns that are short-term.

Budgetary Policies That Are Sound Governments should strive to implement fiscal policies that are sound, which include competent budget management and the avoidance of excessive deficits. In order to decrease the need for governments to resort to printing money in order to meet budget gaps, it is possible for governments to maintain fiscal discipline.

Transparency and Accountability: It is imperative that governments be transparent in their dealings with financial matters, and that officials be held accountable for the decisions they make. Building trust in the monetary system and lowering the possibility of hyperinflation being caused by covert activities are both outcomes that can be achieved through transparency.

Cooperation on a Global Scale: In a worldwide economy, it is vital to have international cooperation in order to address economic imbalances and avert hyperinflation. Providing aid to nations that are experiencing economic crises and coordinating fiscal and monetary policies are two examples of the kinds of collaborative actions that might be undertaken.

Increasing the Diversification of Revenue Sources In order to lessen their reliance on a single industry, such as the oil or commodity markets, governments should increase the diversity of their revenue sources. Increasing economic resilience and decreasing the economy's susceptibility to shocks from the outside world are both possible outcomes of diversification.

Frameworks for Effective Regulation It is vital to implement and enforce regulatory frameworks that are effective in order to prevent financial malfeasance and corruption. Assuring the stability of the financial system and preventing excessive risk-taking can be accomplished with the assistance of a robust regulatory environment.

When hyperinflation occurs, it wreaks havoc on economies, leaving behind a path of economic destruction, social upheaval, and geopolitical ramifications of its aftermath. One of the most prominent factors that has contributed to hyperinflationary events throughout history is the excessive creation of money by the government. This highlights the importance of careful fiscal and monetary policy. The lessons of the past must be learned by governments, and they must put into action measures to restrict the hazards that are linked with the rise of the money supply without any checks and balances.

For the purpose of avoiding the dangers of hyperinflation and fostering economic stability, a complete approach must include essential components such as independent central banks, transparent financial practices, and international cooperation. To protect the economic well-being of nations and the people who live in them, it is of the utmost importance that we have a solid understanding of the constraints that are placed on the printing of money by the government as we negotiate the complexity of the global economy.

Chapter 1

Introduction

Hyperinflation is a phenomenon that stands out as a catastrophic occurrence in the annals of economic history. It is a storm that sweeps away the economic underpinnings of nations and leaves in its wake a landscape of financial disaster and social instability. It is the dangerous practice of the government generating money without any restrictions that is at the core of this destructive power. Hyperinflation is a severe economic phenomenon that can have far-reaching repercussions. It is characterized by a stratospheric rise in prices that leads to a quick devaluation of a nation's currency. In this essay, we will begin an investigation of hyperinflation by deconstructing its roots, analyzing historical examples of occasions in which it occurred with terrible results, and delving into the essential issue regarding the restrictions that must be set on government printing in order to prevent such economic calamities.

The Origins of Hyperinflation: An Investigative Look at the Causes

In order to gain an understanding of hyperinflation, it is necessary to disentangle the complex web of circumstances that contribute to the phenomenon's origin. There are a number of key catalysts, one of which is the unfettered increase in the money supply. This rise in the money supply is a dangerous route that, when adopted by governments, results in a decline in the real value of the currency. This increase in the money supply, if it is not supported by a proportionate growth in the production of goods and services, will result in an imbalance, which will then set off a chain reaction of events that will catapult an economy into the dangerous regions of hyperinflation.

Mismanagement of the government's finances is another significant aspect that contributes to the development of hyperinflation. When governments are forced to deal with budgetary shortfalls and resort to spending levels that are not sustainable, they find themselves at a crossroads of financial desperation. Within the context of an effort to close the financial gap, the printing press emerges as a solution that is both tempting and dangerous. The repercussions of such activities manifest themselves as an economic story that is entrenched in inflationary pressures that spiral out of control.

On the other hand, the origin of hyperinflation is not the only thing that may be attributed to economic mistakes. It is a powerful accelerant when there is a lack of faith in the national currency, which is frequently made worse by political instability or weak monetary policy.

As a result of citizens losing faith in the stability of their money, a cascade effect occurs, in which people rush to spend their currency before it depreciates even further, adding fuel to the fires of hyperinflation.

In addition, the failure of monetary policy becomes a significant contributor to the problem. When political pressures threaten the independence of central banks, which are tasked with the responsibility of maintaining price stability and economic equilibrium, these institutions have the potential to accidentally become vehicles of hyperinflation. It is possible to set the setting for a dangerous dance with hyperinflation by implementing ineffective policies or interventions that disregard the fundamentalists of the economy.

Examples of hyperinflation throughout history: a historical tapestry

Throughout the course of history, there have been numerous times in which hyperinflation has taken place, leaving behind scars that serve as lessons for subsequent generations to learn from. Notable among these accounts is the hyperinflation that occurred in the Weimar Republic in the early 1920s. This event has left an indelible mark on the collective memory of historians and economists.

Germany found itself in the position of having to shoulder the burden of devastating war reparations in the aftermath of World War I. The German government, which was confronted with an impossible financial situation, resorted to employing a magnitude of money printing that had never been seen before. Following this, a hyperinflationary spiral ensued, which caused prices to skyrocket into the stratosphere and rendered the German mark worthless. Citizens were witnesses to the surreal scene of lugging wheelbarrows full of money in order to purchase essential items. This image, which will forever symbolize the catastrophic power of hyperinflation, was witnessed by the citizens.

Over the course of time, the reverberations of hyperinflation spread throughout the world, eventually reaching the African nation of Zimbabwe in the late 2000s. Mismanagement of the economy, political instability, and contentious land reforms all came together to produce the perfect storm by combining their forces. The Zimbabwean dollar, which was once a symbol of national pride, has been unable to withstand the effects of hyperinflation, and the decision to issue trillion-dollar notes is a demonstration of how severe the problem has become.

During more recent times, Venezuela was confronted with an economic calamity that was comparable. Millions of people's savings and means of subsistence were depleted as a result of hyperinflation, which was caused by a confluence of circumstances, including economic incompetence, corruption, and the collapse of oil prices.

The bolivar in Venezuela experienced a precipitous decline, leaving the country's population to contend with the harsh reality of hyperinflation.

Hyperinflation is not a relic of the past; rather, it is a recurring specter that can haunt societies when fundamental economic principles are abandoned. These historical cases serve as sharp reminders that hyperinflation is not obsolete.

Insights into the Effects of Hyperinflation: The Cost of the Problem

The repercussions of hyperinflation are not limited to the world of economic theory; rather, they make their way into the very fabric of society and nations. Due to the fact that hyperinflation disturbs the normal functioning of markets, the first victim of hyperinflation is frequently the stability of the economy. In a situation in which prices are increasing at a rate that has never been seen before, it is difficult for businesses to establish prices that are stable, and customers are compelled to make a mad dash to spend their money before its worth decreases even further.

In hyperinflationary environments, the erosion of wealth becomes a recurrent subject for the landscape. As a result of the disappearance of the true value of investments, pensions, and savings, both individuals and businesses are left suffering from poverty. As a result of the disintegration of the concept of a stable store of value, individuals are looking for refuge in alternative assets or foreign currencies, which further exacerbates the depreciation of the national currency.

On the other hand, the effects of hyperinflation extend beyond the realm of economics and into the social and political fabric of a nation. When citizens, who are struggling to cope with the decline in their purchasing power, express their dissatisfaction through demonstrations, strikes, and acts of civil disobedience, social unrest has the potential to become a tangible potential danger. Because people are having trouble meeting their fundamental requirements, the disintegration of social order becomes a possible result, which in turn creates the conditions for political instability.

In addition to this, the effects of hyperinflation are not limited to the borders of individual nations. Due to the interwoven nature of our global economy, the effects of hyperinflation have the potential to ricochet all over the world. There is a possibility that trade links will be disturbed, that fluctuation will occur in the financial markets, and that overseas investors would struggle with uncertainty. Furthermore, the tentacles of hyperinflation reach beyond the nation that is experiencing it, highlighting the necessity of a concerted effort to limit the potential global impact of this phenomenon.

Limiting the amount of money that the government prints is an imperative

Given the severity of the repercussions, it is clear that there is an absolute necessity to place restrictions on the amount of printing that the government can do. There is a question that needs to be answered: how can countries successfully traverse the perilous seas of fiscal and monetary policy in order to avoid the shadow of hyperinflation that is ever-present? A holistic approach that incorporates economic restraint, institutional safeguards, and international collaboration is the key to finding the answers.

When it comes to the structure of a resilient monetary system, the establishment and maintenance of independent central banks emerge as a cornerstone. The ability to create and implement monetary policies that are founded on economic fundamentals rather than transient political expediency is afforded to a central bank that is autonomous and operates without regard to short-term political considerations. It is impossible to stress the significance of ensuring that the independence of the central bank is protected, as it acts as a barrier against the temptation of governments to resort to the printing of money in order to provide instant relief that is ultimately unsustainable.

A further pillar in the fortress against hyperinflation is the implementation of fiscal policies that are sensible. It is imperative that governments take a methodical approach to the administration of their budgets in order to prevent the accumulation of large deficits, which could lead to the temptation to resort to the printing press. By adhering to fiscal restraint, governments can lessen the need to rely on inflationary measures to fill budget shortages. This is because inflationary methods are generally more expensive.

Within the context of this attempt, transparency and accountability seem to emerge as guiding principles. Governments are obligated to be open and honest about their financial affairs, making information that is both understandable and easily accessible to the general public. In order to cultivate a culture in which economic stewardship is not merely a political weapon but rather a grave responsibility, policymakers need to be held accountable for the decisions that they make.

Within the framework of the strategy to prevent hyperinflation, international cooperation emerges as an essential individual component. There is the potential for the acts of a single nation to have far-reaching consequences in a global economy that is interconnected. It is possible to construct a web of resilience that reduces the risk of hyperinflation spreading across borders through collaborative efforts in the coordination of fiscal and monetary policies, the exchange of best practices, and the provision of aid to nations that are experiencing economic crises.

Diversifying the sources of revenue is a realistic strategy that may be taken to improve the economic resilience of a country. Countries with a high degree of dependence on a particular industry, such as the oil or commodities industry, are more susceptible to the effects of shocks from the outside world. Creating a more resilient and adaptive economic structure can be accomplished through diversification, which can help decrease this risk.

In order to avoid financial malfeasance and corruption, which can worsen economic instability, effective regulatory frameworks play a significant role in the prevention of these practices. The maintenance of trust in the monetary system and the prevention of excessive risk-taking, which could lead to hyperinflation, are both dependent on the existence of a financial sector that is heavily controlled.

The prospect of hyperinflation, which has the potential to destabilize economies and plant the seeds of social and political discontent, highlights the necessity of putting restrictions on the amount of money that the government can issue. In the process of navigating the complexity of the global economy, the lessons that we have learned from previous instances of hyperinflation encourage us to proceed with caution and to put into action measures that will ensure the resilience of the economy.

It is necessary to exercise vigilant oversight and adhere to solid economic principles in order to prevent hyperinflation from occurring, which has its origins in the unchecked expansion of the money supply and in the mishandling of the budget. The Weimar Republic, Zimbabwe, and Venezuela are just a few examples of historical events that serve as powerful reminders of the catastrophic potential of hyperinflation and the urgent need for preventative measures.

The imposition of limits on the printing of government currency is not a lonely undertaking but rather a multidimensional approach that incorporates the autonomy of central banks, fiscal policies that are solid, transparency, accountability, international collaboration, diversification of revenue sources, and regulatory frameworks that are effective. When taken as a whole, these components constitute a solid structure that protects nations from the treacherous voyage into hyperinflationary territory.

While we are confronting the difficulties of the present and the future, the essence that is clear is that the maintenance of economic stability and the protection of the buying power of nations' currencies require a vigilant commitment to responsible economic governance. The restrictions placed on the printing power of the government, which are incorporated within the framework of appropriate fiscal and monetary policies, serve as a defense mechanism against the devastation caused by hyperinflation. They also provide a way to achieve economic resilience and long-term prosperity.

1.1 Overview of Hyperinflation

It is a rare but severe economic phenomenon that is defined by an exceptionally quick and often accelerating increase in the general price level of goods and services within an economy. Hyperinflation is a relatively uncommon but severe economic phenomenon. The consequence of this is that the currency of a country will devalue, which will ultimately result in a loss of faith in the monetary system. Throughout the course of history, hyperinflationary episodes have been inextricably linked to economic mismanagement, fiscal irresponsibility, and a breakdown in the normal functioning of a nation's monetary system. In this overview, the most important aspects of hyperinflation are discussed, including its causes, implications, historical examples, and the steps that have been attempted to reduce the impact of extreme inflation.

The Factors Affecting Hyperinflation

An Overabundance of Money Supply:

Hyperinflation can be attributed to a number of factors, one of the most important of which is an excessive increase in the money supply that is far faster than the expansion of the economy's goods and services. Price increases are the outcome of an imbalance between supply and demand, which occurs when governments resort to creating money without discrimination, thus flooding the market with currency. When more money is used to purchase the same quantity of products, the value of the currency decreases at a quick rate.

Poor Financial Management and Fiscal Policies: Poor fiscal policies and financial management are frequently the root causes of hyperinflation. For the purpose of compensating for financial shortages, governments may resort to activities such as deficit spending, excessive borrowing, or the printing of money. When these measures are not supported by economic policies that are sustainable, they have the potential to lead to a spiral of inflation.

The stability of a nation's currency is directly proportional to the level of confidence that people have in that currency. In the event that there is a lack of faith in the currency as a result of causes such as political instability, economic uncertainty, or perceived mismanagement, hyperinflation may be caused. There is a possibility that people would rush to spend their money in anticipation of greater depreciation, which will exacerbate the pressures of inflation.

The failure of monetary policy contributes to hyperinflation. Monetary policies that are either ineffective or poorly implemented are a contributing factor. The ability of central banks to exercise control over the amount of money in circulation is undermined when they are unable to preserve their independence and instead give in to political pressures. Hyperinflation can also be caused by monetary policies that are not sound, such as maintaining interest rates at very low levels for an excessively extended period of time.

The Repercussions of Excessive Inflation

One of the most significant consequences of hyperinflation is the disruption of the normal functioning of an economy, which ultimately results in anarchy in the market. The establishment of stable prices is a challenge for businesses, and customers are confronted with uncertainty over the future value of their money. In a situation characterized by hyperinflation, economic planning becomes extremely difficult to accomplish.

The Deterioration of Wealth The most immediate and observable effect of hyperinflation is the depletion of wealth. Savings, pensions, and investments all experience a dramatic decline in their actual worth. The citizens discover that the money they have worked so hard to earn may be used to purchase fewer products and services, which results in a deterioration in their general standard of living.

Social Unrest: As a result of citizens bearing the brunt of economic suffering, hyperinflation frequently corresponds with social unrest. It is possible that people would show their unhappiness with the deteriorating economic conditions by participating in demonstrations, going on strikes, and causing civil unrest. Both social cohesiveness and political stability are under jeopardy as a result of its current state.

Although hyperinflation is essentially a national phenomena, its ramifications can transcend beyond boundaries. This is because hyperinflation can have global implications. In an economy that is interconnected on a global scale, the effects of hyperinflation in one country can have an effect on trade links, disrupt financial markets, and generate uncertainty for international investors.

Examples of Hyperinflation Throughout History

It was the Weimar Republic in Germany from 1921 to 1923

Hyperinflation, which occurred under the Weimar Republic, is one of the most infamous episodes in the history of the world. Following the conclusion of World War I, Germany was forced to pay enormous amounts of war reparations. The German government resorted to extensive money printing in order to unleash hyperinflation, which resulted in the currency being insignificant and almost worthless. The citizens were witnesses to the odd situation of having to carry wheelbarrows full of cash in order to purchase essential items.

Zimbabwe (2007-2009): In the late 2000s, Zimbabwe was plagued by hyperinflation, which was caused by a confluence of factors including economic incompetence, political instability, and disputed land reforms. It was at this time that Zimbabwe experienced the printing of trillion-dollar notes, which led to the Zimbabwean dollar being almost worthless.

In recent years, Venezuela has been experiencing hyperinflation as a consequence of economic mismanagement, corruption, and the drop of oil prices. This situation is expected to continue until 2021. A severe economic crisis that left millions of Venezuelans battling with poverty brought on by hyperinflation was brought about by the collapse of the bolivar, which was the currency of Venezuela.

In order to reduce hyperinflation, the government should impose printing restrictions

Central Banks That Are Independent:

It is essential to establish and preserve the autonomy of central banks in order to reduce the amount of intervention that the government has in monetary policy discussions. As opposed to making judgments based on short-term political considerations, a central bank that is equipped with autonomy is able to make decisions based on economic realities.

Sound Fiscal Policies: It is imperative that governments implement sound fiscal policies, which include prudent budget management and the avoidance of excessive deficits by the government. In order to decrease the need for governments to resort to printing money in order to meet budget gaps, it is possible for governments to maintain fiscal discipline.

Transparency and Accountability: Governments should embrace transparent financial processes and provide clear information to the public when it comes to financial matters. For the purpose of cultivating a culture in which economic stewardship is regarded as a solemn responsibility, policymakers need to be held accountable for the decisions they make.

International Cooperation: In a worldwide economy, it is vital to have international cooperation in order to address economic imbalances and avert hyperinflation. Providing aid to nations that are experiencing economic crises and coordinating fiscal and monetary policies are two examples of the kinds of collaborative actions that might be undertaken.

Diversification of money Sources: In order to lessen their reliance on a single industry, such as the manufacturing of commodities or oil, governments should diversify the sources of money they receive. Increased economic resilience and decreased susceptibility to shocks from the outside world can be achieved through diversification.

Regulatory Frameworks That Are Effective It is vital to implement and enforce regulatory frameworks that are effective in order to avoid financial malfeasance and corruption. Assuring the stability of the financial system and preventing excessive risk-taking can be accomplished with the assistance of a robust regulatory environment.

1.2 Historical Cases of Hyperinflation

Hyperinflation, a condition that affects the economy and is defined by an unmanageable spike in prices and the quick devaluation of a nation's currency, has left indelible impressions on the pages of history. This essay dives into past instances of hyperinflation, analyzing the factors that led to these economic catastrophes, the effects they had, and the lessons that can be learned from them for the foreseeable future. All of these cases serve as a cautionary tale, highlighting the disastrous impact that unbridled inflation can have on economies and communities. From the hyperinflationary nightmare that occurred in the Weimar Republic to the more recent crises that have occurred in Zimbabwe and Venezuela, each event serves as an example.

The Weimar Republic (Germany, 1921-1923)

Contextualization of the Past:

The Weimar Republic, which emerged in the aftermath of World War I, was confronted with the formidable problem of economic restoration in the midst of social upheaval and war reparations. The Treaty of Versailles imposed significant reparations on Germany, which made the country's economic problems even worse.

The vast creation of money to satisfy war reparations was the primary cause of hyperinflation in Weimar Germany. This was the principal impetus for hyperinflation in Germany during the Weimar Republic. Due to the fact that the government was confronted with unachievable financial demands, it resorted to printing an unprecedented quantity of currency, which resulted in a rapid devaluation of the German mark.

The adverse effects of hyperinflation in Weimar Germany included the disruption of the economy and the discontentment of the society. Prices skyrocketed to previously unimaginable heights, rendering the currency almost completely worthless.

The citizens were forced to endure the unfathomable ordeal of transporting wheelbarrows full of cash in order to purchase essential items. It was a time when savings vanished, enterprises went out of business, and the middle class fell into poverty.

Lessons That Will Last Forever The hyperinflation that occurred during the Weimar Republic serves as a sharp warning of the disastrous results that might result from unregulated money printing. Specifically, it highlights the need for fiscal responsibility, the value of solid economic policies, and the necessity of maintaining the independence of central banks in order to prevent political meddling in areas pertaining to monetary policy.

Zimbabwe (2007-2009)

The historical context: Zimbabwe, which was once regarded as the breadbasket of Africa, was confronted with economic issues, including contentious land reforms and political instability. The government, which was led by Robert Mugabe, struggled with both corruption and mismanagement of the country's finances.

The causes of hyperinflation include economic mismanagement, political instability, and land changes that impacted agricultural productivity. All of these factors contributed to the phenomenon of hyperinflation. In order to finance budget shortfalls, the government resorted to printing money, which further exacerbated the inflationary pressures that were already present.

The hyperinflation that Zimbabwe experienced resulted in the country issuing notes consisting of one trillion dollars. Both the value of the currency and the prices increased at the same time. Citizens were confronted with a precarious economic situation, which included shortages of essential commodities and services. Poverty and unemployment were widespread problems in the country as a result of hyperinflation.

Lessons That Will Last Forever The situation in Zimbabwe exemplifies the devastation that can result from periods of political upheaval and the significance of preserving economic stability. This highlights the importance of having a diverse range of revenue sources, open financial processes, and efficient regulatory structures in order to prevent financial wrongdoing and corruption.

Venezuela (from 2016 to 2021)

Venezuela, which was formerly a nation that was rich in oil, was confronted with economic difficulties as a result of the precipitous drop in oil prices. During the time that President Nicolás Maduro was in office, the government struggled with issues of popular unrest, incompetence, and corruption.

The Causes of Hyperinflation The hyperinflation that Venezuela experienced was the consequence of a confluence of factors, including the collapse of oil prices, government corruption, and poor economic management. It was necessary for the government to print money in order to offset budget gaps, which contributed to the pressures of hyperinflation.

As a result of hyperinflation in Venezuela, the country is currently experiencing a serious economic crisis. The bolivar had a rapid depreciation, and the inhabitants battled to overcome the poverty that was caused by hyperinflation. The country's plunge into economic turbulence was defined by a number of factors, including social unrest, shortages of essential products, and deteriorating infrastructure.

Lessons That Will Last Forever The situation in Venezuela highlights the precarious position of economies that are primarily dependent on a single industry, such as the oil industry. In order to correct economic imbalances and avert hyperinflation, it places an emphasis on the necessity of having a diverse range of revenue sources, honest financial processes, and international cooperation.

Hungary (1945-1946)

The historical context: Following World War II, Hungary was confronted with the difficulties of reconstruction and economic instability. The devastation caused by war, in conjunction with transitions in governmental power, laid the groundwork for hyperinflation.

The causes of hyperinflation The funding of wartime deficits and reparations payments were the primary factors that led to the hyperinflation that Hungary experienced. The government resorted to printing money, which resulted in the inflationary pressures that were already there.

Consequences: The hyperinflation that Hungary experienced led to economic chaos being observed. There was a sharp decline in the value of the currency, and prices skyrocketed. As the citizens' money became worthless, they were forced to endure hardships. A significant factor that contributed to political instability was the hyperinflationary crisis.

In the instance of Hungary, the hazards of financing wartime deficits through the printing of money are brought to light, and these lessons will endure. It places an emphasis on the significance of fiscal responsibility, economic planning, and the requirement for international cooperation in order to forestall the disastrous effects of hyperinflation.

The episodes of hyperinflation that have occurred throughout history serve as cautionary stories, providing economic planners and nations in general with lessons that are of great value. The effects of unregulated money production are severe and far-reaching, resulting in economic upheaval, social unrest, and permanently scarring the national psyche. These consequences are dire and far-reaching.

The lessons that may be learned from these historical situations include the necessity of ensuring that central banks continue to maintain their independence, the implementation of fiscal policies that are solid, and the diversification of sources of revenue. When it comes to averting the return of hyperinflation, the most important factors to consider are transparent financial processes, strong regulatory frameworks, and international cooperation.

In the midst of nations grappling with economic issues and searching for sustainable paths to prosperity, the historical instances of hyperinflation serve as stark reminders of the dangers of fiscal recklessness and the significance of ensuring the stability of national currencies. It is possible for societies to strive to construct resilient economies that are able to resist the strains of time and successfully navigate the intricacies of the global economic landscape if they pay attention to these teachings.

1.3 Importance of Understanding Limits on Money Printing

The concept of money printing, which is also formally known as monetary expansion or quantitative easing, has garnered a significant amount of attention in the realm of economic policy and central banking, particularly during periods of economic uncertainty. At the same time that the ability to create money provides policymakers with a tool to address a variety of economic challenges, it is essential to have a solid understanding of the limitations and consequences that are associated with the unchecked printing of money. This essay examines the significance of having a clear understanding of these boundaries as well as the potential consequences that could result from exceeding them.

It is instructive to examine historical examples where the consequences of unchecked monetary expansion were pronounced in order to gain an appreciation for the significance of understanding one's ability to set limits on the printing of money. One example that is particularly noteworthy is the hyperinflation that occurred in the Weimar Republic in the early 1920s. In an effort to address war reparations and fiscal challenges, the German government resorted to printing an excessive amount of money, which ultimately resulted in a catastrophic devaluation of the currency. The citizens were subjected to a steady increase in prices, a reduction in their savings, and economic upheaval. The hyperinflation that occurred during the Weimar Republic serves as a cautionary tale that emphasizes the importance of responsible monetary policy.

Managing a nation's money supply and putting monetary policy into action are two of the most important responsibilities that fall under the purview of central banks. When it comes to economic growth, employment, and price stability, the primary objective is typically to maintain price stability. Central banks are required to exercise caution in order to avoid unfavorable outcomes, despite the fact that controlled money creation is a tool that can be used to achieve these goals.

Increased Inflationary Pressures: Unrestricted money printing is associated with a number of primary concerns, one of which is inflationary pressures. On the other hand, inflation happens when the supply of money is greater than the demand for goods and services, which ultimately results in an increase in prices across the board. It is common practice to consider moderate inflation to be normal in an economy that is expanding; however, hyperinflation can reduce the purchasing power of currency, which can have negative consequences for both individuals and businesses.

When it comes to understanding the limits of money printing, it is necessary to acknowledge the delicate balance that exists between promoting economic activity and preventing inflation from spiraling out of control. Central banks make use of a wide range of instruments, such as adjustments to interest rates and open market operations, in order to manage the dynamics of the money supply and effectively control inflationary pressures.

In addition to the restrictions placed on the printing of money, the accumulation of public debt is another aspect of the restrictions. An increase in debt levels that is not sustainable poses long-term challenges, despite the fact that monetary expansion can provide temporary relief by financing government expenditures. It is possible that the accumulation of debt will result in increased interest payments, which will in turn distract the government from spending on other essential areas, which could ultimately lead to a fiscal crisis.

In order to gain an understanding of the restrictions placed on the printing of money, it is necessary to conduct a thorough cost-benefit analysis of the policies implemented by the government. It is possible that an excessive reliance on money creation to fund budget deficits could provide relief in the short term; however, in the long run, this could have negative consequences for the financial health of a nation.

Currency Depreciation and Exchange Rates: Unrestrained money printing can be a factor in currency depreciation, which in turn can have an effect on international trade and exchange rates. As a result of a weaker currency, imports become more expensive, which may result in trade imbalances and economic distortions.

In order to develop an understanding of the limitations of money printing, it is necessary to acknowledge the interconnectedness of domestic monetary policy with the dynamics of the global economy.

As a result of the fact that currency devaluation can lead to competitive devaluations and trade tensions, central banks are required to take into consideration the implications of their actions on the international stage. Not only does a nuanced approach to monetary policy take into account the domestic economic goals, but it also takes into account the broader implications for the continuity of the global economy.

There is a strong correlation between the confidence and trust of a nation's citizens and the stability of the nation's currency. This is true both within the nation's borders and in the international community. To keep people's faith in the monetary system, it is necessary to have a solid understanding of the restrictions placed on the printing of money. It is possible for people to lose faith in the value of their currency, which can then lead to a loss of confidence in financial institutions, which in turn undermines the efficiency of monetary policy.

In order to cultivate public trust, central banks are required to communicate in a responsible and transparent manner. A clear communication about the rationale behind decisions regarding monetary policy, the commitment to maintaining price stability, and the acknowledgment of the limits on money printing all contribute to the development and maintenance of confidence in the financial system.

The importance of understanding the limits on money printing is highlighted by historical examples of nations that struggled with the consequences of imprudent monetary policies. These examples were used to illustrate the lessons that can be learned from learning from economic history. The hyperinflation that Zimbabwe experienced in the late 2000s was caused by an excessive amount of money printing, which ultimately resulted in the downfall of the country's currency and severe economic difficulties. In the pursuit of economic goals, these events bring to light the necessity for policymakers to draw lessons from the past and proceed with caution.

Striking a Balance: Recognizing that there are restrictions on the amount of money that can be printed does not mean that its usefulness is excluded. In point of fact, monetary expansion that is well-calibrated and under control can be an effective tool for addressing economic challenges, particularly during times of recession or financial crisis. In order to avoid the pitfalls that are associated with an excessive reliance on money creation, it is essential to strike a balance between using monetary policy to stimulate economic activity and avoiding the pitfalls.

It is impossible to overstate the significance of having a solid understanding of the limitations placed on the printing of money in the context of economic policy. There are inherent risks and consequences associated with monetary expansion, despite the fact that it has the potential to serve as an important tool in addressing economic challenges. When it comes to harnessing the benefits of controlled money creation without succumbing to the pitfalls of unchecked inflation, debt accumulation, and loss of trust in the monetary system, policymakers, central bankers, and the general public all need to recognize the delicate balance that is required.

A comprehensive understanding of economic history, a dedication to transparency, and an acknowledgment of the interconnectedness of global financial markets are all necessary components of a nuanced and well-informed approach to monetary policy. It is possible for nations to harness the power of money creation in order to foster economic stability and sustainable growth if they navigate the complexities of monetary policy with the prudence and foresight necessary.

Chapter 2

The Printing Press Paradox

One of the most significant turning points in human history was when Johannes Gutenberg, in the 15th century, invented the printing press. This clever invention revolutionized the production of information, as well as the dissemination and consumption of that information. Additionally, the printing press was responsible for a number of unintended consequences, despite the fact that it was crucial in the development of literacy, the dissemination of information, and the acceleration of social and cultural revolutions. The complex relationship that exists between development and contradiction has been given the name "the Printing Press Paradox" in recognition of its complexity. In this essay, I will attempt to delve into the varied nature of this contradiction by investigating the beneficial and negative effects that the printing press has had on society, culture, politics, and the human mind.

Historically, the origins of the printing press

Before going into the contradiction, it is necessary to have a solid understanding of the historical setting and the origins of the printing press. The mechanical movable-type printing press is generally attributed to Johannes Gutenberg, a German inventor, who is credited with developing the device about the year 1440. This ground-breaking innovation made it possible to produce books and documents in large quantities, which in turn made information more accessible to a wider audience with more ease. The printing press was a break from the difficult and time-consuming process of hand-copying manuscripts. It made it possible to reproduce written content in a way that was both quick and cost-effective.

Influences that are Beneficial to the Printing Press

One of the most notable good effects of the printing press was the democratization of knowledge. This was the most significant positive impact. Before the introduction of the printing press, books were extremely scarce, extremely expensive, and primarily reserved for monasteries, universities, and the upper class. People from all different social strata were given the opportunity to educate themselves as a result of the printing press, which made books more affordable and available to a wider audience.

The printing press was a significant factor in the Renaissance, which was a period of tremendous cultural, artistic, and intellectual revival. The printing press was in large part responsible for the Renaissance. There was a rebirth of interest in study and inquiry that was fostered by the dissemination of scientific information and ancient writings.

Scholars, artists, and intellectuals were able to share their ideas with a wider audience, which helped to cultivate an environment that enabled intellectual curiosity and innovation.

During the 16th century, the printing press was an essential component of the theological reformation that was taking place at the time. The 95 Theses, which were written by Martin Luther and included criticisms of the policies of the Catholic Church, were widely circulated through printed pamphlets, which sparked a movement that ultimately resulted in the foundation of Protestantism. In addition to contributing to the variety of religious thought, the ability to disseminate other religious beliefs posed a challenge to the monopoly that the Church held over religious thought.

The printing press was also responsible for the expansion of scientific information, which led to the advancement of scientific understanding. It is possible for scientific treatises, discoveries, and hypotheses to be disseminated among researchers at a faster rate, which would encourage a collaborative approach to having an understanding of the natural world. The acceleration of scientific communication was a significant factor in laying the framework for the subsequent Scientific Revolution.

The printing press has a number of unfavorable effects

Sensationalism and information overload: As printing technology evolved, the sheer volume of printed material grew. This led to an increase in sensationalism. Despite the fact that the proliferation of information was beneficial for the diffusion of knowledge, it also resulted in an excessive amount of information. It became increasingly impossible to police the quality and veracity of content, and information that was either sensationalized or erroneous made its way into the public sphere.

Political Manipulation and Propaganda: The printing press evolved into a powerful instrument employed for the purposes of political manipulation and propaganda. It was understood by those in positions of authority and political power that it had the potential to influence public opinion, spread ideas, and consolidate control. The press was frequently utilized to propagate information that was either biased or misleading, which contributed to increased political discontent and conflicts.

The democratization of knowledge was a beneficial element; nevertheless, it also led to the loss of old cultural gatekeeping systems. This was a consequence of the democratization of information. The authority of institutions that had historically controlled the flow of information, such as the Church or monarchies, was eroded. Examples of such institutions include nations. This weakening of centralized power had impacts on cultures that were both liberating and destabilizing at the same given time.

The printing press was a significant contributor to the phenomenon of social fragmentation since it allowed for the dissemination of a wide variety of theories and viewpoints. Communities that were formerly united by a common set of beliefs have found themselves confronted with a multitude of ideologies that are in direct opposition to one another. Despite the fact that it encouraged intellectual development, this diversity also planted the seeds for social strife and polarization.

Putting the Printing Press in the Context of Modern Times

Even if it has taken on a different shape, the paradox of the printing press continues to exist in the present period. The proliferation of the internet and other forms of digital media has further sped up the process of knowledge distribution, which has amplified both the positive and negative elements of the paradox that was initially presented.

Digital Revolution: The internet and other developments in communication technology have been the driving forces behind the digital revolution, which has ushered in a new era of information transmission. When compared to what was achievable with the printing press, the pace at which information flows today is significantly faster. Platforms for social networking, blogs, and online news outlets all contribute to the continuous and instantaneous flow of information that is available online.

The issue of misinformation, which has historical origins dating back to the time of the printing press, has taken on new dimensions in the digital age. Fake news and misinformation are two examples of this dilemma. The ease with which false information may be manufactured, circulated, and amplified on the internet presents a huge challenge to the reliability of the sources of information. The phrase "fake news" has evolved into a catch-all phrase that refers to information that is either manufactured or deceptive and has the potential to spread quickly and widely.

The advent of the digital era has made it easier for people all over the world to communicate with one another and share their cultures. This is analogous to the positive effects that the printing press had been responsible for. It is now possible for people from different regions of the world to instantly communicate their thoughts, viewpoints, and works of art with one another. One consequence of this interconnectedness is that the world has become more cosmopolitan and culturally varied.

Worries surrounding Privacy and Digital Surveillance The advent of the digital age has provided rise to worries surrounding privacy that have never been seen before. The capacity to follow and monitor the activities of individuals while they are online has given rise to ethical problems regarding the appropriate balance between personal freedom and security precautions. Concerns such as data breaches, identity theft, and spying have emerged as important topics of discussion in relation to the digital landscape.

The Printing Press Paradox is a phenomenon that is both complicated and long-lasting, and it highlights the ambivalence that is associated with the progression of technology. The invention of the printing press brought about unexpected effects, despite the fact that it was a game-changer in terms of the distribution of information and played a significant part in determining the path that history would take. Despite the fact that the digital revolution has amplified both the beneficial and negative sides of information transmission, the paradox continues to exist in the present setting.

Before we can successfully manage the complexity of the digital age, it is very necessary to do an in-depth analysis of the impact that new technologies have had on society, culture, and the autonomy of individuals. The lesson that can be learned from the Printing Press Paradox is that the democratization of information comes with responsibilities that must be taken into consideration. Within the context of the ongoing narrative of technological advancement, one of the most challenging challenges that continues to be faced is the task of striking a balance between openness and control, encouraging variety of thought while protecting against manipulation.

2.1 How Money is Created by Governments

Money is an essential component of contemporary economies since it functions as a medium of commerce, a unit of account, and a store of value. Many people make use of money on a daily basis, but the complexities of how it is created are still a mystery to the majority of people. A fundamental part of this process is played by governments, and it is vital to have an awareness of how money is created in order to have a complete comprehension of the dynamics of economic systems. Within the scope of this article, the methods by which governments generate money are investigated, including the historical development of the process, the function of central banks, and the effects that the generation of money has on economies.

Perspectives on the Past:

It is possible to trace the beginnings of money generation all the way back to the history of the practice of trading. On the other hand, as economies became more complicated, barter systems were shown to be insufficient. In an effort to make commerce more accessible, governments started issuing currencies, which were often in the form of coins. A further transformation of the environment of money generation has occurred over the course of time as a result of the move to paper money and, more recently, digital currencies.

Central banks and the use of fiat currency:

There is a common practice in modern economies to refer to money as "fiat money." In contrast to commodity money, which encompasses precious metals like gold and silver, fiat money does not possess any inherent worth and is not supported by any tangible asset. As an alternative, its value is derived from the faith and confidence that individuals have in the government that is responsible for issuing it. When it comes to the regulation of the money supply, central banks, which are the monetary authorities of the majority of countries, play an essential role.

The Methods Used to Generate New Money:

A method known as fractional reserve banking describes the mechanism by which governments generate new money. Commercial banks are only obligated to keep a small portion of their deposits as reserves, which enables them to lend out the majority of the funds that they come into possession of. When a bank extends credit in the form of a loan, it practically generates fresh money. This is because the amount that is loaned is deposited into the account of the borrower, which contributes to the total amount of money that is available. This process is amplified by the multiplier effect, which contributes to the expansion of the money stock in the economy as a whole.

As for the Function of Central Banks:

It is the responsibility of a nation's central banks to protect the nation's monetary policy. In order to exert influence over the state of the economy, they manage the money supply as well as interest rates. Open market operations are one of the methods that central banks use to monitor and control the amount of money in circulation. These operations involve the buying and selling of government securities. In addition, commercial banks are subject to reserve requirements that are established by central banks, which has an impact on the former's capacity to generate new money through lending.

In addition to unconventional monetary policies, quantitative easing refers to:

It is possible for central banks to use unorthodox monetary policies, such as quantitative easing, while the economy is experiencing turbulent times. In order to inject money directly into the economy, this includes the purchase of financial assets, which are often bonds issued by the government. Despite the fact that these policies have the potential to assist in the stimulation of economic activity, they also raise concerns over inflation and the stability of the monetary system over the long run.

There are two types of inflation:

An essential component of monetary policy is the link that exists between the production of new money and the rate of inflation.

Inflation that is under control is sometimes seen to be a characteristic of economies that are in good health; nevertheless, inflation that is excessive can cause the value of money to decrease, which has a negative impact on both consumers and businesses. On the other hand, deflation, which is defined as a persistent reduction in the overall level of prices, presents its own unique set of issues, one of which is the possibility of a decrease in economic activity.

Potential Consequences for Economies:

There are significant repercussions for both the growth and stability of the economy related to the process of money production and the management of that money by governments. Monetary policies that are effective strive to achieve a balance between fostering economic activity and preserving price stability. There have been numerous instances throughout history of hyperinflation or financial crises that have demonstrated the potential for financial instability to result from either poor management or a lack of knowledge of the dynamics at play.

Having an understanding of the process by which governments generate money can provide valuable insights into the operation of contemporary economies. This essay has studied the intricate network that underpins the monetary systems that we negotiate on a daily basis, beginning with historical viewpoints and moving on to the function of central banks and the methods of money production. It is highly possible that the dynamics of money creation will experience more modifications as economies continue to expand and technology continues to shape financial landscapes. This development will make the dynamics of money creation an ever-fascinating subject for research and analysis.

2.2 Mechanisms of Currency Printing

A painstaking procedure that is governed by a combination of precision, security, and advanced technology, the generation of physical currency, which is frequently considered to be the lifeblood of economies, is a process that is outlined below. The processes that are involved in the transformation of raw materials into tangible notes and coins are investigated in depth throughout this essay, which dives into the mechanics that are used in the printing of currency. The journey of currency displays a seamless blend of artistry, technology, and security measures from the beginning through the conclusion, beginning with the design phase and ending with the distribution.

Creating Value in Currency:

The design phase is the first step in the process of creating currency. During this phase, the central bank of a nation works along with professional artists, engravers, and designers to develop banknotes that are both visually appealing and secure. For the purpose of preventing counterfeiting, the design contains elaborate patterns, images of historical figures, national symbols, and innovative security elements.

Holographic strips, watermarks, microprinting, and color-shifting inks are some examples of the security elements that can be included in these documents. These features make it extremely difficult to replicate the document.

Picking the appropriate materials to use:

When the design has been completed, the selection of materials becomes an important factor to take into consideration. Historically, banknotes were printed on cotton paper, which offered both longevity and a distinct feel to the material. On the other hand, developments in polymer technology have resulted in the introduction of polymer banknotes in a number of countries. Polymer notes have greater security features, as well as increased durability and resilience to wear and tear due to their composition. When deciding between paper and polymer, there are a number of considerations to take into account, including the cost, the impact on the environment, and the desired longevity of the currency.

Steps in the Printing Process:

The actual printing of banknotes is accomplished using a synergistic combination of intaglio printing, offset printing, and various other specialized printing methods. It is usual practice to utilize intaglio printing, which is distinguished by the presence of raised ink on the surface, for the complex details and portraits that may be found on banknotes. The use of offset printing, on the other hand, is employed for the creation of patterns and colorful backgrounds. There are multiple printing plates made for each color, and the notes go through a number of printing runs in order to get the final design.

Including Safety Measures in the Architecture:

When it comes to the printing process of currency, security measures are an essential component since they act as a deterrent to any attempts at counterfeiting. These characteristics are frequently incorporated into the printing process and may include the following:

Images or patterns that are imprinted into the paper or polymer during the production process are known as watermarks.

Folio strips that include holographic graphics that change their appearance when tilted are referred to as holographic strips.

Text or patterns that are extremely small and difficult to reproduce precisely are examples of microprinting.

Altering the Colors Inks: Inks that exhibit a difference in hue when viewed from a variety of perspectives.

There are thin metallic threads or strips inserted within the banknote that are referred to as security threads.

The Control of Quality:

It is of the utmost importance to guarantee the quality and authenticity of printed currency. Throughout the entirety of the printing process, stringent quality control measures are continuously employed. Automated systems investigate each note for flaws, guaranteeing that only banknotes that are free of any imperfections are sent on to the next stage of processing. The necessity of precision in the creation of currency is highlighted by the fact that any defects or abnormalities are marked for manual scrutiny.

Digitization of Serial Numbers and Signatures:

Additionally, a one-of-a-kind serial number is assigned to each and every banknote during the printing process. This code, which is composed of letters and numbers, is used to keep track of and identify specific notes. The signatures of key authorities, such as the minister of finance and the governor of the central bank, are printed on certain banknotes in addition to the serial numbers that are printed on them. The authority that is responsible for the issuing of the currency is reflected in these signatures, which additionally offer an additional layer of credibility to the currency.

Determining and Organizing:

After the banknotes have been created and examined, they are then subjected to a process that involves cutting and sorting them. The vast sheets of printed banknotes are first sliced into individual notes by specialized equipment, which adhere to the dimensions that have been predetermined. At the same time, the notes are arranged into the bundles according to the denominations that they contain. It is necessary to exercise precision throughout this stage in order to guarantee that all banknotes are of the same size and appearance.

In terms of distribution and packaging:

Following the cutting and sorting of the banknotes, the bundles of banknotes are carefully wrapped and then readied for distribution. The distribution process is supervised by the central bank, which is also known as the designated currency issuer. This ensures that the newly created money is distributed to commercial banks, financial institutions, and ultimately the general population. The logistics of transferring and protecting huge quantities of currency need the implementation of complex security systems in order to prevent theft or access by unauthorized individuals.

Innovations and Obstacles to Overcome:

For the printing of currency, the ongoing development of technology brings a number of opportunities as well as significant obstacles. Despite the fact that the digital era has generated questions about the future of physical cash, the resistance of banknotes against counterfeiting has been enhanced by the use of improved printing techniques and security features. There are alternatives to traditional cash transactions, such as cryptocurrencies and digital payment systems, which raises issues about the continued significance of physical money in the long run.

The process of printing currency is a fascinating journey that combines artistic ingenuity, technological perfection, and stringent security measures. This journey begins with the development of the design and ends with the distribution of the final product. The age-old method of physically generating currency is continuously refined as economies adjust to technology breakthroughs and changing consumer tastes. This technique has been around for a very long time. Not only does having an understanding of these mechanisms provide insights into the tangible features of monetary systems, but it also brings to light the fine balance that exists between innovation and tradition in the world of currency manufacturing.

2.3 Initial Implications of Increased Money Supply

One of the most important factors that determines the dynamics of an economy is the idea of money supply, which refers to the total amount of money that is in circulation within an economy. Alterations in the money supply have the potential to have significant repercussions for areas such as inflation, interest rates, and the overall stability of the economy. The first implications of an expanded money supply are investigated in this essay. The study looks at the potential impacts that an increase in the money supply could have on various parts of the economy as well as the issues that policymakers may encounter when attempting to manage these repercussions.

The Understanding of the Money Supply:

There are many different types of money that are included in the money supply, which is sometimes divided into multiple measures such as M1, M2, and M3. These measurements include demand deposits, physical cash, and other forms of money that are more liquid. There are a number of different avenues through which a rise in the money supply can take place. These include interventions by the central bank, fractional reserve banks, and government expenditure. In the beginning, the effects of such increases are complicated and multi-faceted, and they can have both beneficial and bad resultant effects.

There are pressures of inflation:

An increase in the money supply has a number of immediate ramifications, one of the most obvious of which is the possibility of inflationary pressures.

An rise in the quantity of money available to individuals and businesses results in an increase in their purchasing power, which in turn leads to an increase in the demand for products and services. It is possible for prices to rise, which would lead to inflation, if the economy is unable to meet the increased demand with an equivalent increase in production. The rates of inflation are regularly monitored by central banks, who then make adjustments to their monetary policies in order to keep prices stable.

Regulation of Monetary Policy and Interest Rates:

There is a correlation between an increase in the money supply and interest rates, which have a significant role in determining patterns of investment, borrowing, and spending. It is possible for central banks to undertake contractionary monetary policies as a response to the increasing money supply and the potential threat of inflation. The purpose of these policies is to increase interest rates in order to make borrowing money more expensive, which will ultimately result in a reduction in consumer spending and company financing. On the other hand, a reduction in the money supply could result in expansionary monetary policies, which are measures that try to reduce interest rates in order to encourage economic activity.

The Prices of Assets and the Financial Markets:

It is possible for an increase in the money supply to have an effect on the prices of assets like equities, bonds, and estate. In the event that there is an abundance of money in the financial system, investors may try to increase their returns by investing in a variety of assets, which might result in an increase in the prices of those assets. This occurrence has the potential to play a role in the development of asset bubbles, which occur when the prices of assets exceed their fundamental values. As was seen in historical events such as the fall of the housing market in 2008, the bursting of such bubbles can have significant repercussions for the financial markets as well as the economy as a whole.

In the context of international trade, exchange rates:

Alterations in the money supply have the potential to affect exchange rates, which in turn can have an effect on a nation's ability to compete in international trade. There is a possibility that the national currency will depreciate as a result of a rise in the money supply, particularly when this is coupled by a decrease in interest rates. Although this has the ability to enhance exports by lowering the prices of goods for purchasers in other countries, it also has the potential to raise the prices of imports, which could potentially contribute to trade imbalances. The delicate balance that must be maintained between domestic economic goals and the maintenance of a stable currency rate is a challenge that policymakers frequently face.

Both the Levels of Debt and the Financial Stability:
The amount of debt that an economy carries can be impacted by an increase in the money supply.

When interest rates are lower, which is typically associated with a rise in the money supply, borrowing money might become more appealing. There is a possibility that this will increase economic activity; nevertheless, it also raises concerns about the accumulation of excessive debt, both on the individual and individual government levels. There is evidence that high amounts of debt can be a threat to the stability of the financial system, as was seen in instances of sovereign debt crises.

The Confidence of Customers and of Businesses:
A shift in the money supply can have an effect on the confidence of both consumers and businesses. During times of economic expansion, which are made possible by a rise in the money supply, consumers may experience a greater sense of optimism regarding their financial prospects, which causes them to increase their spending. The same may be said for firms, which might be more likely to invest and grow their operations. On the other hand, if increases in the money supply are seen as unsustainable or inflationary, it can weaken confidence, which in turn can lead to a decline in spending and investment.

The Distribution of Income:
A rise in the money supply might have early repercussions that can also have an effect on the distribution of income within a society. There is a possibility that the impacts will not be uniform, and that specific subsets of the population would suffer larger favorable or unfavorable outcomes. For instance, if pay growth is less than inflation, this can result in a decrease in real incomes for certain individuals. Furthermore, asset price inflation may be a factor in wealth disparity since individuals who have considerable holdings in financial assets are more likely to gain from it than others who do not have such holdings.

Challenges and factors to take into consideration for policymakers:
Guidance for the Future:
It is essential for central banks to communicate their intentions for monetary policy in a clear and concise manner, which is referred to as forward guidance. There is a correlation between transparent communication

and the shaping of expectations among firms, investors, and consumers, which in turn influences their decisions regarding spending, saving, and investing finances.

Using Data to Drive Policies:

When it comes to formulating effective policies, policymakers consistently rely on economic indicators and data. Monitoring inflation rates, employment figures, and other economic indicators in real time enables decision-making that is driven by evidence, which in turn enables prompt adjustments to be made to monetary policy.

A Coordination of the World:

When it comes to a global economy that is interconnected, it is necessary for policymakers and central banks to coordinate their efforts. There is the potential for actions done by one nation to have repercussions for other nations, particularly with regard to the exchange rates and the flow of capital. Coordinated efforts have the ability to reduce the impact of any potential disruptions.

Capacity for Adaptation and Flexibility:

Considering the fluid nature of the economic environment, policymakers must maintain a degree of adaptability and flexibility in their approach. An approach that is universally applicable might not be appropriate, and it might be essential to make modifications in accordance with the particular conditions that are present in each economy.

Strategic Framework for the Long Term:

To address the initial implications of a rise in the money supply, it is necessary to take into mind the policy frameworks that will be in place over the long run. Structural reforms that promote sustainable economic growth, reduce income inequality, and strengthen the resilience of financial systems should be the primary emphasis of policymakers.

Increases in the money supply have the potential to have far-reaching and diverse effects on economies after they are implemented. Policymakers are required to traverse a complicated environment, which includes the possibility for inflationary pressures and changes in interest rates, as well as the influence on asset values, international commerce, and the distribution of income. An continuous problem is to strike a balance between the stimulative impacts of increasing money supply and the risks of destabilizing inflation during times of economic expansion. As economies continue to develop and global factors continue to have an impact on monetary policies, it is essential for policymakers to take a nuanced and data-driven approach in order to successfully traverse the complexity of controlling money supply for the benefit of their respective nations.

Chapter 3

The Domino Effect of Inflation

The phenomena known as inflation, which is defined as the continual increase in the general price level of goods and services, is a phenomenon that has far-reaching implications on economies and organizations. The consequences of inflation spread throughout a variety of industries, causing a domino effect that has an impact on the lives of individuals, corporations, and governments. This phenomenon is analogous to a chain reaction. This comprehensive examination digs into the intricate web of the domino effect of inflation, analyzing its origins, manifestations, and the complex interaction of economic variables that amplify its effects.

What You Need to Know About Inflation:

Before digging into the domino effect, it is necessary to have a solid understanding of the nature of inflation and the factors that contribute to it. Inflation can originate from a number of different factors, such as demand-pull inflation, cost-push inflation, and built-in inflation. An increase in prices is the result of demand-pull inflation, which happens when the aggregate demand for goods and services is higher than the aggregate supply of those goods and services. There is another type of inflation known as cost-push inflation, which is caused by increased production costs, such as increases in wages or the pricing of raw materials. Wage-price spirals are a common cause of built-in inflation. These spirals occur when workers demand greater pay, which in turn leads to increasing production costs and, as a result, higher prices.

The First Domino: The Purchasing Power of Individual Consumers

As the cascade of inflationary effects continues, the impact on the purchasing power of consumers is the first domino to fall. Whenever there is an increase in prices, the actual worth of money decreases, which in turn reduces the purchasing power of customers. Consequently, this results in a decrease in the standard of living for both individuals and households.

People who earn a fixed income, such as retirees who get pensions, are more susceptible to the effects of inflation since their income might not keep up with the rate of inflation, which would reduce their capacity to sustain the same level of consumption.

Deterioration of Real Income:

The decay of real income as a result of inflation is a significant factor that contributes to the domino effect. It is possible for consumers to reduce their discretionary spending when they suffer a drop in their purchasing power. This can have a negative impact on businesses and contribute to a slowdown in economic activity.

Inequality of Income:

Due to the fact that inflation has a tendency to have a disparate impact on various income levels, it can make income inequality worse. Individuals and families with lower incomes may experience the strain more intensely, whilst those with higher incomes may have more flexibility to absorb additional expenditures. The growing disparity between those who are wealthy and those who are struggling to make ends meet is one factor that contributes to social inequalities.

The Field of Business: The Pressures of Costs and the Decision-Making Process:

As the domino effect of inflation continues to move forward, it eventually enters the domain of business, hence presenting new obstacles for established businesses.

An increase in the costs of production:

As a result of growing costs for labor, energy, and raw materials, businesses are facing the additional challenge of increased manufacturing costs. It is possible that these increasing costs will force businesses to either absorb the additional expenses themselves, which will result in decreased profit margins, or pass them on to customers in the form of price hikes, which will continue the circular process of inflation.

Uncertainty and the Decisions Regarding Investments:

One of the factors that contributes to the uncertainty that exists in the corporate climate is inflation. The difficulties that organizations have when making decisions regarding long-term planning and investments can be exacerbated by fluctuating prices and rising costs. It is possible that this uncertainty may result in investments being delayed, capital expenditures being decreased, and an expansion strategy that is more conservative.

Financial Markets and Investments:

Inflation has a domino effect that spreads across the financial markets, influencing investment strategies, asset values, and the behavior of investors throughout the process.

When it comes to bond markets and interest rates:

Interest rates are frequently increased by central banks as a response to inflationary pressures within the economy. There is a correlation between higher interest rates and bond markets, which results in a decrease in the prices of current bonds. It is possible for bondholders to suffer capital losses, which would result in a reassessment of their different investment portfolios.

Equity Markets:

There are a variety of ways in which inflation might impact equities markets.

On the one hand, businesses who are able to pass on additional expenses to customers may be able to keep or even grow their profit margins. Increasing volatility, on the other hand, can be caused by factors such as rising interest rates and uncertainty, which can have an impact on stock prices. There is a possibility that investors will seek sanctuary in assets that have traditionally been seen to be hedges against inflation, such as real estate or commodities.

Inflation and Real Estate:

There is a close connection between the domino effect of inflation and real estate, which is a key component of wealth for a lot of people.

The Inflation of Assets:

It is possible for inflation to play a role in the inflation of asset prices, especially real estate. It is possible that individuals and institutional investors would want to maintain and grow their wealth by investing in tangible assets such as real estate as the value of money continues to fall. It is possible that this increased demand could cause property prices to rise, which will make it more difficult for first-time purchasers to become homeowners.

Mortgage Interest Rates and Relative Affordability:

It is possible that rising inflation may force central banks to raise interest rates, which will have an effect on mortgage rates. Homebuyers may experience a rise in the cost of borrowing money as a result of higher interest rates, which may result in a decrease in affordability and a decrease in demand in the real estate market.

Responses from the Government and Fiscal Policy:

There are several instances in which governments find themselves at the vanguard of the fight against inflation, employing fiscal policies in order to mitigate the effects of inflation.

Interventions by the Central Bank:

The use of monetary policy by central banks is an essential component in the process of controlling inflation. By performing open market operations and making adjustments to interest rates, central banks strive to achieve their goals of controlling inflation and stabilizing economic circumstances simultaneously. The effectiveness of these interventions, on the other hand, is contingent upon a number of factors, such as the factors that are responsible for inflation in the first place and the degree to which consumers and businesses are responsive.

Policy Measures Regarding the Budget:

For the purpose of preventing inflation from spiraling out of control, governments may choose to employ fiscal policy measures.

Adjustments to taxation, spending by the government, and federal subsidies are all examples of these types of initiatives. On the other hand, accomplishing the delicate task of striking the correct balance between boosting economic activity and reducing inflationary pressures is a difficult challenge.

The Social and Political Consequences of the Situation:

The domino impact of inflation has enormous social and political repercussions, which shape public sentiment and influence political landscapes. These ramifications are brought about by the domino effect.

Unrest in the Social Order and Inequality:

As a result of inflation, citizens' purchasing power is being reduced, which may lead to an increase in irritation and discontentment, which could ultimately result in civil upheaval. It is possible for the unequal distribution of the burden of inflation to further fuel frustrations and deepen socioeconomic disparities that already exist.

Political Reactions and the Maintenance of Stability:

In order to successfully navigate the problems posed by inflation, governments need to strike a delicate balance between the implementation of vital reforms and the maintenance of social and political stability. It is possible for political unrest and leadership changes to occur if inflation is not effectively addressed.

Inflation, which may be defined as a persistent increase in the overall level of prices, is the catalyst that sets off a domino effect that is intricate and interrelated, and it has repercussions throughout economies and society. Each stage of the inflationary cascade contributes to a dynamic and ever-changing economic landscape. This includes the issues that are encountered by businesses, financial markets, and governments, as well as the erosion of the purchasing power of consumers. The repercussions are not limited to economic statistics; rather, they extend to the very fabric of societies, having an impact on the dynamics of society, the stability of politics, and the general well-being of individuals. knowledge the complexity of the domino effect is becoming increasingly important for policymakers as they struggle to manage the complexities of inflation. Being able to devise successful measures that promote economic stability and social cohesion in the face of inflationary pressures requires that policymakers demonstrate a knowledge of the domino effect.

3.1 Exploring the Causes and Effects of Inflation

The concept of inflation is a complicated economic phenomenon that has far-reaching effects for individuals, corporations, and governments. An economy is said to be experiencing inflation when there is a persistent rise in the overall price level of goods and services over a period of time to be measured. As a result of inflation, the purchase power of money decreases, which in turn causes changes in consumer behavior, investment patterns, and the overall stability of the economy. The objective of this paper is to investigate the factors that lead to inflation as well as its consequences, with the goal of throwing light on the complex systems that are responsible for this economic phenomenon.

Implications of Inflation:

The phenomenon known as demand-pull inflation is one of the key factors that contribute to inflation. This type of inflation occurs when the total demand for goods and services is higher than the total supply of those goods and services. When there is a surge in consumer spending, company investment, and government expenditure all at the same time, it results in a situation in which demand exceeds supply. Due to the fact that producers are having a difficult time meeting the increased demand, prices have increased.

Cost-Push Inflation: Cost-push inflation is a type of inflation that arises when the costs of production go up, which forces firms to pass on these increased costs to customers in the form of higher prices for goods and services. Cost-push inflation can be caused by a number of factors, including but not limited to rising wages, increased costs of raw materials, and disruptions in supply chain operations. The type of inflation that is being discussed here frequently causes a fall in the profit margins of enterprises, which in turn can lead to a decrease in both output and employment.

Inflation on the Wage-Price Basis or Built-In:

There is a self-perpetuating loop that is known as built-in inflation. This cycle occurs when rising prices lead to demands for higher wages, and higher wages, in turn, lead to greater production costs. Despite the fact that businesses are increasing their prices in order to preserve their profit margins in the face of rising labor expenses, consumers are demanding greater pay in order to deal with the rising cost of living. This repetitive process has the potential to generate a feedback loop, which in turn can fuel inflationary pressures.

Inflation is significantly impacted by monetary issues, which play a particularly important role in the process. There is a possibility that an excessive amount of money will be chasing a limited supply of products if a central bank decides to increase the money supply without simultaneously increasing the amount of goods and services available. Because of this, prices may end up being higher. Alterations in interest rates and the availability of credit can also have an effect on spending habits, which in turn can have an effect on inflationary pressures.

Consequences of the Inflation:

One of the most immediate and apparent effects of inflation is the fall in the purchasing power of money. This decline in purchasing power is one of the most significant consequences of inflation. Individuals and households experience a decline in their level of life as a result of the fact that each unit of currency can purchase a smaller quantity of goods and services as prices continue to rise. Since the purchasing power of people on fixed incomes, such as retirees, decreases with time, this might have a disproportionately negative impact on those individuals.

Inflation is a significant contributor to economic instability because it adds uncertainty into the economy, which makes it difficult for firms to plan and invest for the future. This can lead to an unstable economic climate, which discourages long-term investments and slows economic growth. Price fluctuations that are either sudden or unanticipated can also contribute to this. Consumers' confidence is also impacted by uncertainty, which might result in alterations to their spending patterns.

When there is inflation, central banks frequently respond by increasing interest rates in order to slow down economic activity. This is done in order to prevent more inflation. When interest rates are higher, borrowing money becomes more expensive, which in turn leads to a decrease in businesses' investments and consumer spending. An illustration of the interdependence of inflation and broader economic conditions is provided by the fact that the consequent decline in economic activity can contribute to a slowdown or recession.

Redistribution of Income: Inflation has the potential to have a redistributive influence on both earnings and wealth. There is a possibility that debtors who have loans with fixed rates will gain from inflation because the real worth of their debt will fall. When the purchasing power of their savings decreases, however, savers and creditors may incur losses in real terms. This is because the value of their savings decreases. These dynamics have the potential to contribute to shifts in the distribution of wealth within a society.

Global Competitiveness: The persistent inflation of a country can have an effect on the global competitiveness of that country. It is possible for a nation's exports to become more expensive if the country's inflation rate is higher than that of its trade partners. This can result in a decrease in the nation's ability to compete on the international stage. On a global scale, this can have an impact on trade balances and contribute to economic imbalances already present.

Inflation is a complex economic phenomenon that is impacted by a variety of factors, including those on the supply side and those on the demand side. It is essential for consumers, organizations, and governments alike to have a solid understanding of the factors that lead to and are affected by inflation.

Inflation that is excessive or quick can have a negative impact on economic stability, living standards, and general prosperity. Moderate inflation, on the other hand, is regarded to be a normal component of healthy economic growth. The management of inflation and the maintenance of a robust and sustainable economic environment both need the implementation of efficient monetary and fiscal policies in order to achieve a state of equilibrium.

3.2 Hyperinflation and its Devastating Consequences

A hyperinflationary inflation is a severe form of inflation that is characterized by a rapid and uncontrollable growth in the prices of goods and services, which frequently reaches levels that are considered to be astronomical. The phenomena of hyperinflation is an extreme situation that can have serious repercussions for individuals, businesses, and entire economies. Inflation is a normal economic phenomenon, but hyperinflation is an extreme scenario. In order to shed light on historical occurrences and the long-lasting impact that hyperinflation has had on society, the purpose of this article is to investigate the causes of hyperinflation as well as its disastrous repercussions.

Things that lead to hyperinflation:

Uncontrolled and Excessive Money Supply The fundamental factor that contributes to hyperinflation is the expansion of the money supply that is both excessive and uncontrolled. When a government decides to create money as a means of financing its budget deficits or meeting its short-term obligations, this is one of the possible outcomes. A devaluation of the currency and an increase in prices are the results of a quick input of money into the economy that does not correlate to an increase in the amount of goods and services that are being produced.

Loss of Confidence in the Currency: One of the most common causes of hyperinflation is a loss of confidence in the national currency. When individuals and businesses lose faith in the security of the currency, they look for ways to shift their money into assets that are more stable, such as international currencies, commodities, or tangible items. This further exacerbates the demand for foreign currencies, which in turn puts extra pressure on the currency that is prevalent in the country.

Mismanagement of the fiscal system: Ineffective fiscal policies, such as excessive government spending, budget deficits that cannot be sustained, and inefficient taxation, can all contribute to hyperinflation. In order for governments to fulfill their financial responsibilities, they might resort to the creation of new money, which would result in a vicious cycle of increasing prices and more economic instability.

Shocks to the Economy: Sudden and severe economic shocks, such as wars, political instability, or natural disasters, have the potential to disrupt production and supply systems, which can ultimately lead to a collapse in output. It is possible for hyperinflationary pressures to become more intense when the supply of goods and services decreases while the money supply continues to rise.

Exemplifications of Hyperinflation Throughout History:

The Weimar Republic, which lasted from 1921 to 1923, is often considered to be the most notorious instance of hyperinflation that took place in Germany during the early 1920s. When the Weimar Republic was forced to make payments for reparations following World War I, it resorted to printing a large amount of money. Due to the skyrocketing prices, individuals were required to have wheelbarrows full of money in order to purchase even the most fundamental of items. The hyperinflation that occurred in Weimar Germany had a series of severe effects on both the economy and society. It was a significant factor in the emergence of radical ideologies and contributed to political instability.

Zimbabwe (2007-2009):Zimbabwe was struck by one of the most severe hyperinflations in the history of contemporary financial markets, which occurred in the latter part of the 2000s. The fall of the Zimbabwean dollar was caused by a combination of causes, including political instability, land reforms, and bad economic management. These factors all contributed to the collapse of the Zimbabwean dollar. Almost all of the money was rendered absolutely unusable as a consequence of the soaring costs. The subsequent hyperinflationary crisis resulted in a number of negative outcomes, including the collapse of the economy, the escalation of poverty, and the surfacing of social unrest.

The Hyperinflationary Effects That Have a Devastating Impact:

A quick decline in the purchasing power of the local currency is the most immediate effect of hyperinflation. This is because hyperinflation causes the value of the domestic currency to decrease. A number of people are discovering that their savings and income are becoming practically worthless, which makes it difficult for them to afford even the most fundamental necessities. It is possible for social unrest and a general decline in well-being to result from the poverty and economic hardship that is caused by the situation.

Savings and wealth are both destroyed by hyperinflation, which causes savings to be wiped out and wealth to be eroded. In the event that the value of money continues to fall, persons who are in possession of cash or financial assets that are denominated in the domestic currency will see the actual worth of their savings disappear. People lose faith in traditional banking and investing channels as a result of this, which contributes to the long-term ramifications for the stability of the financial system.

Disruption of Economic Activity Hyperinflation causes disruptions to normal economic operations because it makes it difficult for firms to adjust to the quickly shifting economic landscape. When prices continue to rise in an unpredictable manner, it becomes difficult for enterprises to establish prices, make plans for the future, and obtain financing. There is a decrease in investment and capital formation, which results in a vicious cycle of economic contraction.

Social discontent and Political Instability: The social repercussions of hyperinflation are significant, and they frequently result in widespread social discontent and political instability. It is possible for people's dissatisfaction and fury to boil over into protests and demonstrations as the economic conditions of the people continue to deteriorate. There is a possibility that governments will be tested regarding their legitimacy, and the possibility of political unrest or a change in regime may become more pronounced.

Inability of Governments to offer Necessary Social Services Hyperinflation can make it more difficult for governments to offer social services that are truly necessary. It becomes increasingly difficult for the government to provide funding for essential services such as education, healthcare, and others as the value of the currency continues to decline. The consequences of this are that social inequality is exacerbated, and the vulnerability of marginalized communities is increased.

Repercussions on the Global Economy The impacts of hyperinflation in one nation might have a domino effect on the economy of other nations across the world. Trade disruptions, disruptions in financial markets, and disruptions in the movement of capital can have an impact on adjacent countries and potentially have ramifications for the framework of the international financial system. When hyperinflationary pressures cause trade and investment flows to be distorted, it is possible that global economic imbalances will emerge.

The extreme economic phenomenon known as hyperinflation has the potential to have catastrophic effects on individuals, organizations, and entire nations. Although hyperinflation can be caused by a variety of factors, it is typically the result of a confluence of factors, including mismanagement of the government's finances, a decline in faith in the currency, and economic shocks. There have been instances of hyper-inflation throughout history that serve as cautionary stories, highlighting the far-reaching influence that it has on society and the significance of having strong economic policy. It is necessary to take a holistic approach in order to combat hyperinflation. This approach should include steps to restore confidence in the currency, smart fiscal management, and stable monetary policy. Hyperinflation's repercussions serve as a sharp reminder of the precarious nature of economic systems and the importance of maintaining vigilance in order to protect the stability of the financial infrastructure.

Chapter 4

The Balancing Act: Monetary Policy

The use of monetary policy by central banks is an essential instrument that they employ in order to ensure economic stability and to foster growth that is sustainable. Managing the money supply and interest rates in order to exert influence over economic activity is a component of this strategy. The process of achieving the optimal equilibrium in monetary policy is a difficult endeavor that calls for the thorough study of a wide range of economic indicators and circumstances. This essay looks into the complexities of monetary policy, analyzing its goals, instruments, and obstacles, as well as the delicate balancing act that is required to navigate the always shifting economic landscape.

The Goals of an Effective Monetary Policy:

Maintaining price stability is one of the primary goals of monetary policy, which is one of the primary purposes of monetary policy. The goal of central banks is to limit inflation by altering interest rates and exerting influence over the amount of money in circulation. It is necessary to maintain price stability in order to build trust in the economy, maintain the purchasing power of money, and make it easier to plan for the economy over the long run.

Full Employment: The development of full employment is another important goal that needs to be accomplished. Recognizing that an overly high inflation rate or protracted periods of unemployment can be damaging to the overall economic well-being of a nation, central banks work toward the goal of achieving a balance between inflation and unemployment. To achieve their goal of maintaining optimal employment levels, central banks try to either promote or cool economic activity through the use of interest rate manipulation.

In order to foster economic expansion, monetary policy is an essential component that must be taken into consideration. The ability of central banks to exert influence over interest rates allows them to encourage borrowing and investment, which in turn stimulates economic growth. In the opposite direction, when the economy is experiencing overheating or inflationary pressures, central banks may tighten monetary policy in order to bring the economy down to a more manageable level and prevent unsustainable growth.

Instruments of Monetary Policy:

The interest rate is the key instrument that central banks employ in order to carry out their monetary policy-making responsibilities. Central banks have the ability to impact the cost of borrowing and lending throughout the economy by modifying the policy interest rate. This rate is known as the federal funds rate in the United States and the repo rate in India. A decrease in interest rates has the effect of encouraging expenditure and investment, whilst an increase in interest rates has the reverse impact.

Open Market Operations This refers to the process by which central banks engage in open market operations by purchasing or selling government assets on the open market. By purchasing assets, a central bank is able to infuse money into the banking system, which in turn results in a reduction in interest rates. On the other hand, selling securities removes money from circulation, which results in an increase in interest rates. The operations of open markets contribute to the regulation of the money supply and have an impact on the short-term interest rates.

Reserve Requirements: Central banks require commercial banks to keep a specific percentage of their deposits as reserves. This percentage vary from bank to bank. Central banks have the ability to exert control over the amount of money that banks have available for lending by simply altering the reserve requirements. The availability of money is increased when reserve requirements are lowered, and the opposite is true when reserve requirements are raised.

Forward Guidance: Forward guidance is a method by which central banks express their intentions on future policy. In order to affect expectations and direct economic activity, central banks provide information on the expected future course of interest rates and other policy measures. This information is intended to steer economic conduct. The costs of borrowing money, decisions about investments, and consumer spending can all be affected by forward guidance.

Obstacles Facing Monetary Policy Discussions:

The existence of temporal lags between the actions taken by policy-makers and the effects those actions have on the economy is one of the issues that are associated with monetary policy. When it comes to responding to rapidly shifting economic conditions, it can be challenging for central banks to fine-tune their policy responses due to the presence of recognition lags, implementation lags, and impact lags.

Existence of Uncertainty in the Economic Environment Central banks function within an environment that is characterized by uncertainty.

The data that pertains to the economy might be unstable and prone to modifications, which makes it difficult to provide an accurate assessment of the current health of the economy. Additionally, the role of monetary planners might be made more difficult by unforeseen occurrences, such as financial crises or developments in geopolitical affairs.

Interconnectedness on a Global Scale: In this day and age of globalized financial markets, central banks are required to take into consideration the international repercussions of the decisions they make regarding policy. Monetary policy actions have the potential to influence fluctuations in exchange rates, capital flows, and trade dynamics. As a result, it is necessary for central banks to negotiate the interconnectedness of the global economy.

Striking a Balance: An Approach to Negotiating Trade-Offs:

Inflation and Unemployment Risk When it comes to balancing inflation and unemployment, central banks frequently have to make a choice between the two. At the same time as attempts to enhance employment may add to inflationary pressures, the pursuit of policies that aim to lower inflation may result in an increase in the rate of unemployment. In order for monetary policy to be effective, it is essential to establish a delicate equilibrium between these two goals.

Comparison of Short-Term and Long-Term Considerations Central banks are required to make a comparison between the economic conditions of the short term and those of the long term. It is vital to avoid measures that could threaten the long-term stability of the financial system or contribute to economic imbalances that are not sustainable. Monetary policy can be used to address current economic issues; nevertheless, it is essential to avoid acts that could do either of these things.

The goal of sustaining financial stability must be synchronized with the pursuit of price stability and full employment. This is necessary in order to achieve financial stability. The stability of financial markets is put in jeopardy when interest rates are considered to be low because they can stimulate risk-taking behavior and asset bubbles. There is always the difficulty of finding the optimal equilibrium that will allow for expansion without encouraging an excessive amount of risk-taking.

The Prospects for Monetary Policy in the Future:

The growth of digital currencies and technical innovation brings new difficulties and chances for monetary policy. These new challenges and opportunities are brought about by the same phenomenon. The potential of central bank digital currencies (CBDCs) is being investigated by central banks, and they are also struggling with the consequences of decentralized finance (DeFi) for the conventional financial system.

ESG, or environmental, social, and governance, considerations include the following:

An increasing amount of emphasis is being paid to the incorporation of environmental, social, and governance factors into monetary policy. Discussions about the incorporation of environmental, social, and governance (ESG) factors into policy frameworks have been prompted by the recognition by central banks of the influence that climate change and social inequality have on economic stability.

Communication and Transparency: Central banks have made it a point to continuously work toward improving communication and transparency. A transparent decision-making process and clear communication of policy goals are two factors that can assist in the management of expectations, the development of public confidence, and the improvement of the efficiency of monetary policy.

Monetary policy is a potent and indispensable instrument for central banks, and it plays a significant part in determining the results of economic circumstances. The delicate balancing act that is involved in accomplishing objectives such as price stability, full employment, and economic growth demands a deep grasp of economic dynamics, the capacity to effectively deploy policy tools, and the ability to adjust to changing difficulties. The future of monetary policy is likely to be influenced by technological improvements, environmental considerations, and continued efforts to promote transparency and communication. This is because central banks are currently navigating the intricacies of the modern economic landscape. For the purpose of ensuring the stability and prosperity of economies all over the world, the pursuit of the appropriate equilibrium in monetary policy continues to be an ongoing issue that calls for an approach that is both deliberate and flexible.

4.1 Role of Central Banks in Controlling Money Supply

When it comes to maintaining a nation's economic and financial stability, central banks play a crucial role, and one of their primary responsibilities is to exercise control over the amount of money that is available. The administration of the money supply is an essential component in the accomplishment of macroeconomic goals such as maintaining price stability, ensuring full employment, and achieving sustainable economic growth. The functions of central banks in controlling the money supply, the methods that they use, and the ramifications of effective monetary control on the overall economic well-being are all topics that are discussed in this essay.

The Roles That Central Banks Will Play:
The central banks of a country are often the only entities that are authorized to issue the currency of that nation. As a result of their ability to produce banknotes and coins, they are able to guarantee the honesty and safety of the monetary system. Within the context of regulating the money supply, one of the most basic aspects is the control of the issuing of currency.

Central banks frequently perform the role of banker to the government by managing the accounts of the government, facilitating transactions, and underwriting the debt of the government. Because of this duty, central banks have a major effect over the overall money supply, which is especially applicable in situations where governments engage in deficit financing.

Central banks provide the function of bankers to commercial banks by managing their reserve accounts and offering a variety of financial services. The process of money production within the larger financial system is under the jurisdiction of central banks, which exercise this influence through the regulation and supervision of commercial banks.

Formulation and Execution of Monetary Policy The formulation and execution of monetary policy is perhaps the most important function that is associated with the control of the money supply. In order to accomplish some of its macroeconomic goals, central banks make use of a wide variety of methods and instruments to exert control over interest rates, credit conditions, and ultimately, the money supply.

Controlling the Amount of Money in circulation:
Open Market Operations: Open market operations, also known as OMO, are carried out by central banks through the public market through the purchase and sale of government securities. By purchasing securities, a central bank is able to inject money into the banking system, increasing the amount of money that is available. When securities are sold, money is removed from circulation, which results in a reduction in the amount of money available. Out-of-money operations (OMOs) are a potent instrument that can be used to affect short-term interest rates and to change the overall money supply.

Reserve Requirements: Central banks require commercial banks to keep a specific percentage of their deposits as reserves. This percentage varies from bank to bank. Central banks have the ability to exert control over the amount of money that banks are able to lend by modifying the reserve requirements. Increasing reserve requirements has the opposite effect of lowering them, which is to reduce the amount of money that is available for lending. Lowering reserve requirements results in an increase in the money supply.

The discount rate is the interest rate that commercial banks are able to borrow cash from the central bank directly. It is also known as the discount rate. The cost of borrowing money for commercial banks is influenced by central banks through the discount rate, which is adjusted frequently. One way to increase the money supply is to lower the discount rate, which encourages banks to borrow more money. On the other hand, increasing the discount rate has the opposite effect.

Central banks employ ahead guidance as a tool to manage expectations in the financial markets and among the general public. ahead guidance is also known as forward guidance. The ability of central banks to affect interest rates and expectations, which in turn has an effect on the money supply, can be demonstrated through the signaling of their intentions on future monetary policy measures.

In times of economic stress or financial crises, central banks may turn to unconventional measures such as quantitative easing (QE). QE is an acronym for quantitative easing. The purpose of this is to inject liquidity into the financial system and to lower long-term interest rates. This is accomplished through the purchase of financial assets on a massive scale, such as government bonds and mortgage-backed securities.

The Implications of an Effective Monetary Control System:

The achievement of price stability is one of the key goals of effective monetary management, which is one of the primary purposes of monetary control. By exercising control over the money supply, central banks strive to bring inflationary forces under control. The maintenance of price stability is essential for the preservation of the purchasing power of money, the promotion of economic confidence, and the development of economic growth over the long run.

Maintaining Stability in Interest Rates Central banks are an essential component in the process of maintaining interest rate stability. Through the use of instruments of monetary policy, central banks are able to exert influence on short-term interest rates, which in turn creates stable borrowing costs for households and businesses. The stability of interest rates is beneficial to economic activity as a whole, as well as to investment and consumption.

The ability of central banks to exert influence on the total economic activity, which in turn has an effect on employment levels, is made possible by the control of the money supply for full employment. The objective of central banks is to achieve full employment while avoiding excessive inflation or deflationary pressures. This is accomplished by the adjustment of interest rates and credit conditions.

Stability in Financial Markets: An effective regulation of monetary policy is one factor that contributes to the stability of financial markets.

A significant contribution that central banks make to the prevention of excessive volatility, asset bubbles, and financial crises is the management of interest rates and liquidity. When it comes to the smooth operation of the economy as a whole, the stability of the financial market is absolutely necessary.

Stability of the Currency: The primary objective of central banks is to ensure that the value of the national currency remains stable. Increased international confidence, increased support for trade, and the prevention of disturbances in the foreign exchange markets are all characteristics of a stable currency. In the context of international commerce and economic integration, the stability of currencies is of utmost significance.

Challenges in Managing the Supply of Money:

One of the difficulties that central banks must contend with is the existence of time lags between the implementation of policy actions and the subsequent effects such actions have on the economy. When it comes to properly responding to changes in the economy, it can be difficult for central banks to fine-tune their reactions due to the presence of recognition lags, implementation lags, and impact lags.

Existence of Uncertainty in the Economic Environment Central banks function within an environment that is characterized by uncertainty. The data that pertains to the economy might be unstable and prone to modifications, which makes it difficult to provide an accurate assessment of the current health of the economy. Additionally, the role of monetary planners might be made more difficult by unforeseen occurrences, such as financial crises or developments in geopolitical affairs.

Because of the interconnected nature of the world, central banks are required to take into account the international repercussions of their policy actions. Monetary policy actions have the potential to influence fluctuations in exchange rates, capital flows, and trade dynamics. As a result, it is necessary for central banks to negotiate the interconnectedness of the global economy.

The Prospects for the Policy of Central Banks:

Innovation and Digital Currencies: Central banks are investigating the opportunities and difficulties that are linked with digital currencies. It is possible that the introduction of central bank digital currencies (CBDCs) could result in a transformation of the monetary landscape. These currencies will offer new instruments for managing the money supply and expanding access to financial services.

There is a growing acknowledgment of the impact that climate change has on the stability of the economy, and monetary policy should take climatic climate into consideration. In recognition of the role that monetary policy plays in mitigating climate-related risks, central banks are investigating the various ways in which they might include environmental considerations into their formulation of policy frameworks.

Central banks are placing a greater emphasis on communication and transparency through the implementation of enhanced communication and transparency measures. A transparent decision-making process and clear communication of policy goals are two factors that can assist in the management of expectations, the development of public confidence, and the improvement of the efficiency of monetary policy.

The ability of central banks to exercise control over the amount of money in circulation is an essential component of both efficient monetary policy and stable economic conditions. Central banks have the ability to exert influence over interest rates, lending conditions, and overall economic activity through the utilization of a variety of measures. The consequences of efficient monetary control extend to the consistency of prices, the consistency of interest rates, the consistency of full employment, the consistency of financial markets, and the consistency of currencies.

Central banks are continuing to adapt to evolving economic dynamics, despite the obstacles that are posed by time lags, an uncertain economic environment, and the interconnection of the global economy. The case studies of the financial crisis that occurred in 2008 and the debt crisis that occurred in the Eurozone demonstrate the significance of adaptability and creativity in the process of reacting to specific difficulties.

With an eye toward the future, central banks are investigating the possibility of digital currencies, including climate-related concerns into monetary policy, and placing a greater focus on communication and transparency. The dynamic nature of the global economy and the requirement for novel approaches to the formulation of monetary policy are reflected in the changing role that central banks play in global economic affairs. When everything is said and done, the successful management of the money supply continues to be an indispensable component in the pursuit of the overarching objectives of economic development and stability.

4.2 Tools of Monetary Policy

For the purpose of attaining economic growth and stability, monetary policy is an instrument that is of critical importance. A wide range of instruments are utilized by central banks all over the world in order to exert influence over the money supply, interest rates, and overall economic activity. This essay investigates the wide variety of tools that are utilized in monetary policy, as well as the mechanisms that underlie them and the difficulties that are involved with their execution. Having a solid understanding of these instruments is absolutely necessary in order to know how central banks negotiate the intricate terrain of contemporary economies.

Indicators of Interest Rates:

Policy interest rates are a primary instrument that central banks utilize in order to implement monetary policy. Examples of policy interest rates are the federal funds rate in the United States and the refinancing rate of the European Central Bank. Through the manipulation of these rates, central banks have the ability to affect the cost of borrowing and lending across the whole economy. A decrease in interest rates has the effect of encouraging expenditure and investment, whilst an increase in interest rates has the reverse impact.

The discount rate is the interest rate that commercial banks are able to borrow cash from the central bank directly. It is also known as the discount rate. The discount rate is one of the primary tools that central banks use to exert influence over the cost of borrowing for commercial banks. At the same time that raising the discount rate has the opposite effect, lowering it encourages banks to borrow more money, which ultimately results in an increase in the money supply.

Central banks use forward guidance as a communication technique to affect expectations in the financial markets and among the general public. Forward guidance is also known as forward guidance. Central banks have the ability to influence interest rates and expectations thanks to the signals they send out on their intentions regarding future monetary policy measures. The provision of forward guidance, which offers direction regarding the expected future path of interest rates, assists in the management of expectations and steer the behavior of the economy.

Open Market Operations (OMO):

Market for the Purchase and Sale of Securities as Open Market The operations of the central bank consist of the purchasing and selling of government securities on the open market where they are traded. By purchasing securities, a central bank is able to inject money into the banking system, increasing the amount of money that is available. When securities are sold, money is removed from circulation, which results in a reduction in the amount of money available. Out-of-money operations (OMOs) are a potent instrument that can be used to affect short-term interest rates and to change the overall money supply.

Repurchase Agreements, also known as Repos, are a type of transaction that involves the selling of government securities with the intention of repurchasing such securities at a later time. The management of short-term liquidity in the banking system is made possible by the temporary transfer of securities that central banks are able to oversee. Through the use of repos, central banks have the ability to exert influence over the money supply as well as the short-term interest rates.

Quantitative and Analytical Tools:

The term "quantitative easing" (QE) refers to an unusual method of monetary policy that is utilized during times of economic strain or instances of financial crisis. In order to pump liquidity into the financial system and bring down long-term interest rates, central banks engage in large-scale purchases of financial assets. These may include government bonds and mortgage-backed securities, among other types of financial assets. When conventional means for adjusting interest rates have reached their limits, quantitative easing (QE) is intended to increase economic activity.

In the context of the economy, credit easing refers to the practice of making targeted purchases of particular assets, such as corporate bonds or commercial paper, with the intention of providing support to particular sectors. By taking this strategy, the goal is to improve lending conditions for consumers and businesses in regions where there is a possibility of disruptions in the financial markets.

Requirements for the Reserve:

The adjustment of reserve ratios is a requirement imposed by central banks on commercial banks, which requires them to set aside a specific proportion of their deposits as reserves. The quantity of money that banks are able to lend is influenced by central banks through the process of altering reserve requirements. Increasing reserve requirements has the opposite effect of lowering them, which is to reduce the amount of money that is available for lending. Lowering reserve requirements results in an increase in the money supply.

Instruments of Communication:

Speeches and news Conferences: Officials from the central bank convey their policy goals, economic assessments, and outlooks through the use of speeches and news conferences. These messages offer further insights into the decision-making process of the central bank, which helps to shape expectations in the financial markets as well as among the general public.

Inflation Targeting: Inflation targeting is a communication strategy in which central banks make a public announcement on a certain inflation target. In order to influence expectations and steer behavior in financial markets and among economic agents, central banks attempt to communicate their commitment to sustaining a given level of inflation in a clear and concise manner.

Obstacles Concerning the Implementation of Monetary Policy Instruments:

Time Lags: The presence of time lags is one of the key issues that is related with the implementation of tools for monetary policy.

There are three types of lags that might make it difficult for central banks to fine-tune their reactions to rapidly changing economic conditions: recognition lags, implementation lags, and effect lags.

Unconventional Policies and Boundaries: The utilization of unconventional monetary policies, such as quantitative easing, has resulted in an expansion of the toolset that is accessible to central banks. Concerns have been made, however, regarding the possible adverse implications of these policies, which include the distortion of financial markets, the formation of asset bubbles, and the difficulties associated with unwinding these measures without also causing disruptions.

Because of the interconnected nature of the world, central banks are required to take into account the international repercussions of their policy actions. Monetary policy actions have the potential to influence fluctuations in exchange rates, capital flows, and trade dynamics. As a result, it is necessary for central banks to negotiate the interconnectedness of the global economy.

The Prospects for the Instruments of Monetary Policy:

Currencies in the digital realm and central banks Cryptocurrencies (also known as CBDCs):

Central banks are taking an interest in the proliferation of digital currencies, which includes central bank digital currencies (CBDCs), as a potential field of investigation. Despite the fact that CBDCs have the potential to improve financial inclusion and give new tools for monetary policy, they also present concerns in terms of privacy and security, as well as the possible influence they could have on traditional banking.

Considerations Regarding Climate Change in Monetary Policy Central banks are becoming more aware of the impact that climate change has on the stability of the economy. There are talks taking place on the incorporation of environmental factors into frameworks for monetary policy, the addressing of risks related to climate change, and the promotion of sustainable finance initiatives.

The central banks continue to place a greater emphasis on communication and transparency, which has led to a rise in the level of transparency. It is easier to manage expectations, create public trust, and improve the efficiency of monetary policy when there is clear communication of policy aims, economic assessments, and decision-making procedures.

The use of monetary policy tools constitutes the arsenal that central banks employ in order to exert control over the conditions of the economy and accomplish their goals. The complexity of today's economic systems is reflected in the wide variety of tools that are available, such as open market operations, quantitative measures, communication techniques, and interest rate instruments.

The problems that are linked with time lags, unconventional policies, global interconnection, and the ever-changing economic landscape necessitate central banks to consistently adapt and innovate in order to maintain their competitive advantage. Case studies based on the financial crisis of 2008 and the debt crisis in the Eurozone highlight the significance of adaptability and innovation in the process of responding to challenging situations that are one of a kind.

Taking a look into the future, it is possible that the future of monetary policy will involve the incorporation of digital currencies, an increased consideration of climate-related factors, and continued efforts to improve communication and transparency. It is still essential for central banks to make good use of the tools of monetary policy in order to achieve economic stability and to create sustainable growth. This is because central banks are navigating the complex web of economic dynamics.

4.3 The Fine Line Between Stimulus and Overprinting

When it comes to the management of monetary policy, it is a delicate balancing act. Central banks must tread a narrow line between the risk of overprinting money and the stimulation of economic growth. It is vital to implement stimulus measures, such as modifications to interest rates, quantitative easing, and fiscal policies, in order to stimulate economic activity during times of economic slump. The excessive use of these measures, on the other hand, raises concerns about the possibility of inflation, currency devaluation, and other unfavorable outcomes. This essay investigates the complex link that exists between stimulus and overprinting. It also investigates the difficulties, dangers, and tactics that have to be utilized in order to successfully navigate this thin line in order to preserve economic stability.

The Reason Reasons Behind Economic Stimulus:

The purpose of economic stimulus measures is to mitigate the adverse consequences of economic downturns, which can include recessions and financial crises. These actions are aimed to counterbalance the negative effects of economic downturns. The goal of central banks and governments is to increase demand and support overall economic activity. This is accomplished by injecting liquidity into the financial system and promoting spending and investment.

Maintaining Price Stability: One of the primary goals of monetary policy is to maintain price stability, and stimulus measures frequently aim to achieve this goal. There is a possibility of deflation emerging during times of economic downturn. Deflation is characterized by declining prices, which might result in decreased spending and investment. The purpose of the stimulus measures, which include lowering interest rates and engaging in quantitative easing, is to forestall deflation and to keep the rate of inflation consistently constant.

Providing Support for Employment: Another objective of economic stimulation is to provide economic support for employment levels. For the purpose of preventing widespread job losses and mitigating the impact of recessions on people and companies, governments and central banks attempt to stimulate economic activity in order to achieve their goals.

Stimulus Measures:

Alterations to Interest Rates: The principal instrument that central banks employ in order to stimulate the economy is the modification of interest rates. A reduction in interest rates brings to a reduction in the cost of borrowing, which in turn encourages individuals and corporations to borrow money and spend it. Investment, consumption, and total economic activity are all stimulated as a result of this.

Quantitative Easing (QE): Quantitative easing is a method of injecting liquidity into the financial system that involves the purchase of financial assets by central banks. These assets include government bonds and mortgage-backed securities. When conventional monetary policy tools are insufficient to stimulate the economy and interest rates are already at historically low levels, this strategy is notably utilized to stimulate the economy.

Fiscal Policies: Governments also have the ability to undertake fiscal stimulus measures, which may include increased government spending, reductions in tax rates, or direct transfers to individuals and businesses. Through the implementation of these policies, the goal is to increase demand, bolster economic growth, and mitigate the adverse consequences of a recession.

Concerning the Dangers and Obstacles:

As a result of vigorous stimulus measures, the potential for inflationary pressures is the principal risk that is connected with these policies. When there is a rapid expansion of the money supply, there is a possibility that the demand for goods and services may exceed the supply, which would result in an increase in prices across the board. It is imperative that central banks regularly monitor inflation expectations and alter their policies in accordance with such expectations.

Devaluation of the Currency Excessive stimulus measures, particularly those that involve large-scale asset purchases, have the potential to result in a devaluation of the national currency. There are potential repercussions for international trade that can arise from a lower currency, including a reduction in export competitiveness and the creation of imbalances in trade ties.

Asset Bubbles: Stimulus measures, particularly in situations where interest rates are at an all-time low, have the potential to contribute to the emergence of asset bubbles. There is a possibility that investors who are looking for larger returns would participate in speculative activities, which could cause the values of assets such as stocks, real estate, or cryptocurrencies to rise. The collapse of these bubbles has the potential to have devastating repercussions for the economy.

The implementation of aggressive stimulus measures may be associated with potential threats to the stability of the financial system. A situation in which interest rates are extremely low can encourage financial institutions to engage in risk-taking behavior that is excessive, which can result in the accumulation of vulnerabilities within the financial system. This has the potential to cause disruptions in the financial markets as well as catastrophic crises.

Strategies for Walking the Fine Line:

Forward Guidance: Forward guidance is a method that central banks employ to communicate their objectives and expectations for policy implementation to the general public. The management of expectations, the guiding of economic conduct, and the prevention of excessive speculation are all contributed to by clear communication regarding the future course of interest rates.

Making Decisions Based on Data: In order to make well-informed choices, policymakers rely on the data and indicators that pertain to the economy. When it comes to establishing the optimal level of stimulus required to sustain economic growth without overheating the economy, central banks are guided by data on inflation, employment, and other economic factors.

Stimulus Measures May Be Reduced Gradually Central banks may reduce their stimulus measures gradually as economic conditions improve in order to avoid making sudden modifications that may potentially disrupt financial markets. Utilizing this strategy makes it possible to have a more seamless transition and lessens the likelihood of market instability.

Macroprudential Policies: In order to address certain risks in the financial system, such as excessive credit expansion or asset bubbles, central banks and regulatory bodies may choose to enact macroprudential policies. It is the intention of these measures to strengthen the resilience of the financial system and to reduce the likelihood of potential dangers.

Taking a Look Into the Tomorrow:

Digital Currencies and Innovation: The proliferation of digital currencies, which includes central bank digital currencies (CBDCs), has opened up new avenues for the implementation of monetary policy. CBDCs have the potential to supply central banks with additional tools that would allow them to conduct stimulus measures while also resolving concerns regarding financial stability and currency devaluation.

Global Cooperation: Given the interrelated nature of the global economy, it is absolutely necessary for central banks to work together and coordinate their actions. Approaches that involve collaboration in the management of stimulus measures have the potential to help prevent spillover effects, eliminate currency tensions, and contribute to the stability of the global economy.

Integration of Environmental Considerations There is a growing interest in the incorporation of environmental, social, and governance (ESG) considerations into discussions regarding monetary policy. For the purpose of incorporating climate-related risks and sustainable finance concerns into their policy frameworks, central banks are now investigating various approaches to do so.

It is necessary for central banks to traverse complicated economic landscapes with expertise and accuracy in order to avoid overprinting and the tiny line that separates stimulus from overprinting. When it comes to reducing the effects of economic downturns, stimulus measures are absolutely necessary. However, it is imperative that careful consideration be given to the dangers associated with inflation, currency devaluation, asset bubbles, and financial instability.

The tactics that are utilized by central banks, including as forward guidance, data-driven decision-making, progressive tapering of stimulus, and macroprudential measures, are of utmost importance in order to preserve the delicate balance. It is expected that the future of monetary policy will be shaped by the incorporation of digital currencies, increased global collaboration, and the consideration of environmental considerations. This will present central banks all over the world with new difficulties and opportunities as the global economy continues to develop.

Chapter 5

The Illusion of Endless Wealth

The allure of unending prosperity is a seductive idea that has frequently penetrated the manner in which economic thought and policy decisions are considered. Throughout the course of human history, the assumption that resources are boundless and that economic expansion may go on endlessly has been the driving force behind the quest of progress and wealth. In spite of this, it is absolutely necessary to analyse this illusion in light of the fact that societies are currently struggling with environmental problems, social inequality, and the limited availability of resources. By putting light on the economic, environmental, and social realities that challenge the concept of boundless prosperity, this essay investigates the complexities of the illusion of endless affluence and discusses the implications of this delusion.

Facts Regarding the Economy:

limitless Resources: The idea of limitless resources is frequently used as the basis for the misconception that one may amass an infinite amount of money. However, the resources of the Earth, which include fossil fuels, minerals, and land that may be used for agriculture, are limited. The strain that is being placed on these resources is becoming more and more visible as populations continue to increase and consumption habits become more intense. This calls for a reevaluation of economic models that are dependent on expansion that is unending.

Externalities and Environmental Costs: Conventional economic models frequently fail to take into account the environmental costs that are connected with economic operations. The extraction of resources, the creation of industrial goods, and the generation of waste all contribute to the degradation of the environment, the expansion of climate change, and the reduction of biodiversity. The assumption that the development of riches can take place without having any negative effects on the health of the world is called into question by the fact that these externalities are included in the true cost of economic expansion.

Inequality and Unsustainable expansion: Although economic expansion has been a contributor to general prosperity, it has frequently contributed to the worsening of social inequities. There are differences in income, education, and access to resources as a result of the fact that the advantages of growth do not necessarily reach all segments of society. When it comes to long-term economic stability and well-being, models of growth that are not sustainable and that continue to perpetuate inequality are not favorable.

Observations Regarding the Environment:

Climate Change and Resource loss: The delusion of unending riches is in direct opposition to the harsh reality of climate change and the loss of resources. Emissions of greenhouse gases created by human activities are a contributor to global warming, which in turn causes climate events to occur more frequently and with greater severity. At the same time, the excessive exploitation of natural resources puts ecosystems and biodiversity at jeopardy, which in turn threatens the basic foundations upon which sustained economic activity is built.

Loss of Ecosystem Services Ecosystem services, which include the purification of air and water, pollination, and soil fertility, are essential to human well-being and economic activities. Agricultural production, public health, and overall resilience are all negatively impacted when ecosystems are degraded, which puts these services at risk. Those who believe in the concept of unending affluence fail to recognize the interdependence that exists between economic prosperity and the state of environmental systems.

Environmental Limits to Growth: The idea of planetary boundaries proposes that there are crucial environmental thresholds that, if exceeded, could result in irreparable damage to the environment being caused by human activity. These limits include restrictions on the loss of biodiversity, changes in land use, the utilization of freshwater resources, and the cycles of nitrogen and phosphorus. When these boundaries are exceeded, the capacity of the Earth's systems to sustain human societies over the long term is put in jeopardy.

The Realities of Society:

When confronted with the harsh reality of wealth disparity, the illusion of unending money is shattered. Inequitable distribution of wealth is a phenomenon that has been observed. There is no guarantee that an increase in economic growth would result in an improvement in the standard of living for everyone. In many instances, the effects of growth are concentrated in the hands of a small number of individuals, which exacerbates existing socioeconomic inequalities and undermines the possibility of achieving sustainable development.

Impacts on Society and Culture Rapid economic expansion frequently results in widespread social and cultural shifts, which can be disruptive to the communities that are affected by them. The deterioration of traditional ways of life and the weakening of communal ties can be a consequence of urbanization, migration, and the commercialization of cultural assets. It is possible to have a loss of cultural diversity and social cohesion as a consequence of the chase of unending money without taking into consideration implications for society.

In terms of health and well-being, the unrelenting pursuit of economic growth can have a negative impact on the health and well-being of individuals.

The environmental repercussions of industrialization, pollution, and the exhaustion of natural resources can all play a role in the development of health problems. In addition, the stress and inequity that are connected with economic practices that are not sustainable can have a significant impact on both the mental health of individuals and the overall well-being of society.

Reconsidering the Existing Context:

The transition to sustainable development is necessary because it is necessary to acknowledge the illusion of infinite wealth. This shift in paradigm is necessary in order to achieve sustainable development. To do this, it is necessary to acknowledge the interdependence of the economic, environmental, and social components, and to work toward achieving a balanced approach that satisfies the need of the present without jeopardizing the capacity of future generations to fulfill their own requirements.

Circular Economy and Resource Efficiency: The transition to a circular economy places an emphasis on reducing waste, reusing materials, and recycling in order to extend the lifespan of resources. In addition to lowering the negative effects that economic activities have on the environment, embracing resource efficiency also poses a challenge to the linear model of production and consumption, which is a factor that contributes to the depletion of resources.

Green technology and Innovation: It is vital to make investments in green technology and to stimulate innovation in order to decouple economic progress from the degradation of the environment. Pathways to economic prosperity that do not compromise the health of the world can be attained through the utilization of environmentally friendly technologies, sustainable agricultural methods, and renewable energy sources.

In order to achieve sustainable development, it is necessary to place a level of importance on social fairness and inclusive growth. Policymakers have a responsibility to address systemic disparities in order to fulfill their responsibility of ensuring that the benefits of economic progress are distributed more fairly among various populations. This involves providing everyone with access to economic possibilities, healthcare, and educational opportunities.

International Cooperation:

When it comes to achieving sustainable goals, international cooperation is necessary since the issues that are posed by the illusion of infinite affluence are of a global nature and require worldwide cooperation. Initiatives such as the Sustainable Development Goals (SDGs) of the United Nations give a framework for countries to collaborate in order to achieve common goals. These goals include the elimination of poverty, the protection of the environment, and the inclusion of social groups.

Environmental Diplomacy and Conservation: The efforts that are made to conserve the environment and engage in environmental diplomacy are extremely important in the process of tackling global concerns. Developing a future that is both robust and sustainable requires the implementation of collaborative projects that aim to preserve biodiversity, fight climate change, and encourage the use of resources in a sustainable manner.

In the face of the harsh realities of a planet with limited capacity and interrelated systems, the illusion of infinite affluence, which is fueled by the belief in limitless resources and perpetual economic expansion, comes into conflict with the harsh reality. The problems that are faced on the economic, environmental, and social fronts highlight the necessity of a paradigm shift toward sustainable development. This is a kind of development in which the pursuit of prosperity is balanced with a profound respect for the boundaries of the Earth and the well-being of all of its people.

By reevaluating economic models, adopting circular economies, investing in environmentally friendly technology, placing a priority on social fairness, and fostering global collaboration, societies have the ability to go beyond the illusion of unending prosperity and construct a future that is more sustainable, resilient, and inclusive. The realization that true wealth encompasses not just the accumulation of material goods but also the preservation of the environment, the maintenance of social harmony, and the promotion of intergenerational equity is essential for successfully navigating the complexity of the 21st century.

5.1 The Misconception of Unlimited Money Printing

In particular, the concept of infinite money printing has been a source of concern and confusion, particularly in relation to the policy of the monetary system. A common misunderstanding that occurs as a result of the actions taken by central banks, such as quantitative easing and unconventional monetary policies, is that there are no restrictions placed on the amount of money that can be created. The purpose of this paper is to dissect the complexity of unrestricted money printing by investigating the facts of monetary policy, the function of central banks, and the potential implications of misperceptions in relation to this essential part of economic management.

The Importance of Comprehending Monetary Policy

The execution of monetary policy is largely dependent on the activity of central banks, which play a crucial role in this process. The maintenance of price stability, the achievement of full employment, and the advancement of economic growth are frequently among their principal goals. A wide variety of tools and instruments are utilized by central banks in order to exert influence over the money supply, interest rates, and overall economic activity in order to accomplish these objectives.

Tools of Conventional Monetary Policy Adjustments to policy interest rates, such as the federal funds rate in the United States or the refinancing rate issued by the European Central Bank, are examples of conventional monetary policy tools. Central banks attempt to exert influence over the costs of borrowing money, as well as investment and spending in the economy, through the manipulation of these rates.

Monetary Policy Instruments That Are Not Traditional Central Banks will turn to unconventional measures in times of economic crisis or when traditional tools are shown to be ineffective. Quantitative easing, sometimes known as QE, is one of these tools. It involves the purchase of financial assets, such as government bonds or mortgage-backed securities, with the intention of injecting liquidity into the financial system.

Quantitative Easing and the Supply of Money:

The purpose and mechanism of quantitative easing are sometimes misunderstood as "unlimited money printing" due to the unorthodox nature of the practice and the scale at which it is implemented. The objective, on the other hand, is to solve particular economic issues, such as pressures toward deflation or a liquidity trap. Central banks generate new money using electronic means and then use that money to buy financial assets. This results in an increase in the money supply and serves as a potential boost for the economy.

It is essential to acknowledge that quantitative easing is not a permanent injection of money into the economy. This is because of the nature of the program, which is temporary. Those assets that were purchased are currently being retained on the balance sheet of the central bank, and the intention is to progressively unwind these positions as the economic conditions continue to improve. The fact that these actions are only temporary sets them apart from the common misunderstanding that they will create money in an endless and indefinite fashion.

Limitations on the Production of New Money:

Inflationary Pressures: The potential for inflationary pressures is the primary limitation that is placed on the ability to print unlimited amounts of money. There is a possibility that prices will increase if the money supply grows at a rate that is excessively rapid in comparison to the expansion of goods and services in the economy. The goal of central banks is to find a balance between promoting economic activity and avoiding excessive inflation. They do this by carefully monitoring inflation expectations and working toward this goal.

Interest Rates and Inflation Expectations: Both interest rates and inflation expectations are influenced by central banks through the usage of interest rates. It is possible for central banks to implement measures to tighten monetary policy, including hiking interest rates, when it is predicted that inflation would grow beyond a target level.

In order to avoid a self-fulfilling cycle of rising prices and to ensure that prices remain stable, it is essential to manage inflation expectations.

Credibility of Central Banks The credibility of central banks is an essential component in determining the efficiency of the monetary policies their institutions implement. In the event that markets and the general public lose faith in the competence of a central bank to control inflation, this can lead to a decline in trust in the currency and ultimately result in economic conditions that are unpredictable. In order to preserve their credibility, central banks are required to communicate their dedication to maintaining price stability.

The Facts Regarding the Independence of Central Banks:

Political Independence: In order for central banks to properly carry out their monetary policy objectives, they are frequently permitted a certain degree of independence without being subject to political influence. Having this independence is essential in order to make judgments that are based on the fundamentals of the economy rather than on considerations of politics in the short run. On the other hand, this does not include unrestricted freedom or insulation from the scrutiny of the public.

Accountability and Transparency: Central banks are answerable to the public and policymakers, despite the fact that they function independently from one another. In order for central bank activities to function well, it is necessary to have procedures for accountability, frequent reporting, and transparency in communication. In order to improve the efficiency of monetary policy, public trust in the decision-making process is absolutely necessary.

Concerning the Repercussions of Misconceptions:

Variability in the Market: Misconceptions about the ability to print endless amounts of money can be a contributor to market volatility. It is possible for investors to experience erratic market behavior, asset bubbles, and rapid fluctuations in investor mood if they have the perception that central banks are pursuing policies that are not sustainable.

There is a possibility that concerns regarding the endless production of money could have an effect on the value of currencies. It is possible for a currency to depreciate if the general public loses faith in the stability of a currency as a result of what they perceive to be an excessive amount of money being created. On the other hand, this may have repercussions for the stability of the economy and for international commercial transactions.

It is possible that the belief in endless money creation could stimulate excessive risk-taking behavior in the financial markets, which could lead to asset bubbles and misallocations.

It's possible that investors may participate in speculative behaviors, which could result in the generation of asset bubbles. The bursting of these bubbles can lead to market corrections, financial instability, and the misallocation of resources, among other unfortunate outcomes.

How to Deal with the Complicated Situation:

Clarity and Communication: In order to remove the belief that central banks have the ability to print endless amounts of money, they must convey their policies in a clear and concise manner. It is important to have clear communication in order to effectively manage expectations, provide direction to market participants, and guarantee that the general public is aware of the objectives and constraints of monetary actions.

Decision-Making That Is Informed By Data Central banks derive their decisions from data and economic indicators in order to make informed choices. Decision-making that is driven by data guarantees that monetary policies are flexible to changing economic conditions. This enables central banks to calibrate their actions based on information that is current at the moment.

Adaptability and Flexibility: Because the economic environment is constantly shifting, it is essential for central banks to maintain their ability to be flexible and adaptive in their approach. Emergencies that were not anticipated, such as financial crises or pandemics on a global scale, call for solutions that are both creative and prompt in order to preserve economic stability.

Looking Ahead to the Future:

The emergence of digital currencies, including central bank digital currencies (CBDCs), provides new aspects to the landscape of monetary policy. This is a result of the fact that digital currencies are becoming increasingly prevalent. The implications of digital currencies for monetary policy, financial stability, and the economy as a whole are being considered by central banks as they investigate the possible advantages and difficulties associated with the use of digital currencies.

Incorporating Climate Considerations into Monetary Policy The incorporation of climate considerations into talks regarding monetary policy is gaining popularity. For the purpose of addressing climate-related risks and promoting sustainable financing, central banks are investigating several methods. A more comprehensive comprehension of the interdependence of economic and environmental sustainability is reflected in the consideration of environmental factors in monetary policy.

The misunderstanding that there is no limit to the amount of money that can be printed originates from a lack of comprehension of the complex structure of monetary policy. In order to ensure economic stability and to foster growth, central banks make use of a variety of tools, while functioning within the boundaries and mandates that have been established. The idea that there is an unlimited supply of money is debunked by the fact that certain initiatives, such as quantitative easing, are only temporary and targeted.

It is essential to have a deep understanding of the complexities of monetary policy and the delicate balance that central banks are required to strike as societies manage the challenges that the economy presents. The ability to communicate effectively, make decisions based on data, and be flexible are essential components in the process of eradicating misunderstandings and developing public trust. When we look to the future, we can see that the incorporation of digital currencies and the consideration of environmental sustainability will define the future landscape of monetary policy. This highlights the necessity of constant innovation and careful economic management.

5.2 Understanding Real vs. Nominal Wealth

For a comprehensive comprehension of the complexity of economic measurement, it is essential to have a firm grasp on the ideas of real and nominal wealth. It is essential to differentiate between nominal and real values when individuals, businesses, and policymakers are evaluating their economic well-being and making decisions with regard to their financial situation. This essay delves into the complexities of real and nominal wealth, illuminating the significance of these notions in the context of economic research, the creation of policy, and the planning of personal finances.

The Difference Between Nominal and Real Wealth:

The value of assets or income that is measured in current, unadjusted monetary terms for the purpose of determining nominal wealth is referred to as nominal wealth. Whether it be the real dollar amount received as income or the face value of financial assets, it is a meaningful representation. Due to the fact that nominal wealth does not take into account fluctuations in the overall price level, it is sensitive to the effects of inflation or deflation.

Real Wealth: Real wealth, on the other hand, takes into account fluctuations in the purchasing power of money over the course of your lifetime. Taking into consideration the effects of inflation or deflation, it is a representation of the value of assets or income expressed in constant dollars. Due to the fact that it takes into account fluctuations in the overall price level, real wealth offers a more precise measurement of economic well-being. This makes it possible to make relevant comparisons across a variety of time periods.

The Effects of Inflation on the Economy:

The overall increase in prices over a period of time is referred to as inflation. Inflation reduces the purchasing power of money, which in turn impacts nominal wealth. The apparent increase in asset values or income may not effectively reflect changes in economic well-being when nominal wealth is measured in the presence of inflation. This is because inflation can cause asset values to rise. There is a possibility that nominal values are deceiving since they do not take into account the decline in the actual value of money.

Adjustment for Inflation Real Wealth: Real wealth takes into account the effects of inflation, which allows for a more accurate depiction of the ways in which economic well-being has changed over time. The concept of real wealth enables individuals and policymakers to determine if there has been an actual increase or decrease in their purchasing power. This is accomplished by describing the values of assets or income in currency that is constant.

The Role of Real and Nominal Variables in Economic Regression Analysis:

When it comes to economic analysis, nominal and real variables are extremely important for determining how well a nation's economy is doing. Gross Domestic Product (GDP) is one of these variables. The nominal gross domestic product (GDP) is a measure of the total value of goods and services produced at the current price level. Real GDP, on the other hand, takes into account fluctuations in the price level and provides a more realistic representation of economic growth.

The difference between nominal and real interest rates is that nominal interest rates calculate the face value of interest payments, but real interest rates take into account changes in the purchasing power of money. Real interest rates offer a more precise measurement of the cost of borrowing money or the return on investments, which enables individuals and organizations to make more informed decisions regarding their finances.

Planning for Financial Investments and Investments:

Investors frequently confront the issue of determining the actual return on their assets, which can have a significant impact on the returns they receive. It is possible that nominal returns will appear to be appealing; nevertheless, when inflation is taken into account, the actual return may be lower than what was anticipated. In order to make educated decisions regarding investments, it is essential to have a solid understanding of the difference between nominal and real values.

The impact of inflation on an individual's future purchasing power is something that should be taken into consideration by those who are involved in long-term financial planning.

It is possible that nominal values, such as predictions of salaries or aims for retirement savings, will need to be converted into real terms in order to guarantee that monetary objectives are in a manner that is consistent with the ever-evolving economic conditions.

Repercussions for Public Policy:

Inflation Targeting and Central Bank Policy: In order to ensure that prices remain stable, central banks frequently establish targeted levels of inflation. Central banks are able to make educated judgments on interest rate policies, money supply, and other monetary tools when they differentiate between nominal and real variables. This allows them to accomplish their inflation targets and encourage economic growth.

Budgeting and Fiscal Policy: Policymakers who are involved in the process of budgeting are required to take into consideration the influence that inflation has on the income and expenditures of the government. In order to guarantee efficient administration of public funds, it is necessary to make adjustments to the nominal budget figures because they might not adequately reflect changes in the actual value of public resources.

Obstacles to Overcome in Measurement:

Accuracy of Price Indices The accuracy of real wealth measurement is dependent on the dependability of price indices that are used to correct for inflation. There are a number of issues that can make it difficult to effectively capture changes in the cost of living, including shifts in consumption patterns, technology developments, and other possible influences.

Subjectivity in Valuation: The process of determining the value of certain assets, such as works of art or real estate, entails a certain amount of inherent subjectivity. It is possible for individual perceptions and the movements of the market to have an impact on the determination of real wealth, which subsequently introduces complexity into the process of measurement.

Considerations for the Future:

In the context of economic measurement, technological breakthroughs, such as blockchain technology, have the potential to influence the manner in which economic transactions are recorded and measured. The accuracy of economic indicators might be improved by the implementation of innovations in data collecting and analysis, which would also involve improvements in the assessment of real and nominal wealth.

Interrelated Economies and Globalization: In a world that is increasingly globalized and where economies are interrelated, it is becoming increasingly vital to have a solid understanding of both real and nominal factors.

There is the potential for the real worth of assets and income to be impacted by fluctuations in exchange rates, trade dynamics, and the conditions of the global economy.

The distinctions between real wealth and nominal wealth are of the utmost importance in the complex landscape of economic measurement. A snapshot of economic indicators expressed in terms of present monetary conditions is provided by nominal values, but real values provide a more accurate reflection of changes in purchasing power over the course of time. In order to successfully navigate economic decisions, financial planning, and policy development, it is essential for individuals, corporations, investors, and policymakers to make sure they have a solid understanding of these ideas.

The effect that inflation has on nominal wealth highlights the importance of taking a sophisticated approach to economic analysis and decision-making. The ability to discriminate between real and nominal values gives individuals and policymakers the ability to make educated choices in an economic landscape that is always shifting. This is true whether they are evaluating the success of the national economy, deciding how to invest their money, or planning for the future. For the purpose of developing economic systems that are both resilient and adaptable, it will continue to be necessary to have a deep grasp of real and nominal wealth as technology, globalization, and economic dynamics continue to undergo further development.

5.3 Inflation's Impact on Savings and Investments

Inflation, which may be defined as the general increase in prices over a period of time, has a significant influence on the purchasing power of individuals, as well as on their financial planning and investing plans. Price increases have a negative impact on the real worth of money, which in turn has an impact on both saves and investments. In this essay, the multidimensional influence of inflation on savings and investments is investigated. The obstacles that inflation presents, tactics for reducing its consequences, and the significance of making educated decisions in the face of economic uncertainty are all discussed in depth.

Understanding Inflation and the Factors That Contribute to It:

Definition and Measurement: The Consumer Price Index (CPI) or the Producer Price Index (PPI) is the most common method for measuring inflation. These indices indicate the average change in the prices of goods and services over a particular time period. It is possible for inflation to be caused by a variety of factors, such as an increase in demand, interruptions in supply chains, higher production costs, or decisions about monetary policy.

Different kinds of inflation include demand-pull inflation, cost-push inflation, and built-in inflation. Inflation can take on a variety of forms, depending on the particular circumstances.

The intricate interaction of elements that contribute to changes in price levels is reflected in the fact that each and every type has its own unique drivers.

The Influence on Savings:

A significant difficulty that is brought about by inflation is the deterioration of the purchasing power of money. This is one of the key challenges that inflation presents. To put it another way, when prices go up, the same amount of money may buy fewer products and services, which means that the value of savings goes down. This has the potential to have significant repercussions for individuals, particularly those who are dependent on fixed incomes or who possess assets that are based on cash.

When comparing nominal interest rates to real interest rates, it is possible that the interest rates that are offered on fixed-income investments or savings accounts may not always keep pace with inflation. Savers experience negative real interest rates when nominal interest rates are lower than the inflation rate. This means that the growth of their savings does not surpass the rise in the cost of living due to the fact that the nominal interest rate is lower than the inflation rate.

Inflation has a variety of effects on various asset classes, and these effects manifest themselves in a variety of ways depending on the type of savings and investment vehicle. When it comes to traditional savings accounts and bonds, particularly those with set interest rates, there is a possibility that real returns will decrease. Certain assets, on the other hand, such as stocks and real estate, as well as commodities, may offer superior protection against inflation. Examples of such assets are real estate and commodities.

Influence on Investments:

Equity Markets and Inflation: Inflation has the potential to bring about a variety of complex effects on equity markets. There is a possibility that some industries, such as commodities or those with pricing power, will benefit from rising prices, despite the fact that corporations may incur greater production costs. When it comes to their investment portfolios, sector allocations, and risk management methods, investors need to take into consideration the potential impact that inflation predictions may have.

Investing in Fixed-Income Securities: Fixed-income assets, such as bonds, are directly affected by inflation. There is a decrease in the purchasing power of the future interest and principal payments that are due from fixed-income instruments when there is an increase in inflation. In the event that the interest collected on bonds does not keep pace with inflation, bond investors run the danger of seeing their investments lose real value.

The use of real assets as inflation hedges Real assets, which include real estate, commodities, and infrastructure, are frequently considered to be inflation hedges. Because of their inherent value, these assets may be able to profit from an increase in price. Those investors who are looking for a way to shield themselves from the deteriorating impacts of inflation may choose to commit a portion of their portfolios to property.

Managing the Risks of Inflation:

Diversification: Diversification is widely recognized as an essential approach for effectively controlling inflationary risks. In order to make their portfolios more resistant to the effects of fluctuating economic conditions, investors can strengthen their portfolios by diversifying their investments across a variety of asset classes, such as real assets, fixed income, and equity investments.

Treasury Inflation-Protected Securities, sometimes known as TIPS, are bonds issued by the United States Treasury that are intended to shield investors from the effects of inflation. Providing a buffer against inflation, the principal value of Treasury Inflation-Protected Securities (TIPS) fluctuates with changes in the Consumer Price Index. Those investors who are interested in gaining exposure to fixed-income may want to think about including TIPS in their portfolios.

Equity Investments in Industries That Are Not Affected by Inflation:

There are some industries that are believed to be more resistant to the effects of inflationary pressures, such as the healthcare industry, the energy industry etc. It is possible that the impact of inflation on equity portfolios can be mitigated by investing in companies that have pricing power, good fundamentals, and the capacity to pass on increasing costs to consumers.

Real Estate and Commodities: Real assets, such as real estate and commodities, such as gold or investments in exchange-traded funds (ETFs) that are tied to commodities, are frequently considered to be hedges against inflation. There is an inherent value to these assets, and they have the potential to offer protection against the deterioration of purchasing power.

Policies of the Government and the Targeting of Inflation:

The responses of central banks show that central banks play a significant part in the management of inflation through the use of monetary policy. The objective of central banks is to continue to preserve price stability and to stimulate economic growth through the implementation of various measures, including adjustments to interest rates. Investors and savers should keep a close eye on the policies of central banks and the potential implications those policies could have for inflation.

Inflation Targeting: As a policy framework, inflation targeting is adopted by a number of central banks internationally. Inflation objectives are a useful tool for guiding decisions on monetary policy, as they provide both transparency and stability. Individuals and investors alike can reap benefits from gaining a grasp of the inflation targets that are established by the central banks of their various countries and remaining updated about these targets.

Obstacles Facing the Management of Inflation:

The unpredictability of inflation dynamics. The dynamics of inflation are impacted by a wide variety of elements, such as the conditions of the global economy, the events that occur in geopolitical affairs, and the changes that occur in structural conditions. Due to the unpredictability of these factors, investors and policymakers face difficulties in effectively anticipating and controlling the risks associated with inflation.

Disruptions in Supply Chains Are Caused by Globalization Globalization has caused economies and supply chains to become interconnected, which has resulted in the introduction of new dynamics into inflationary pressures. Disruptions in the supply chain, such as those that occurred during the COVID-19 pandemic, have the potential to have an effect on the availability and pricing of products and services, which in turn can influence inflationary trends.

Considerations for the Future:

The Accuracy of Inflation Measurement and Technological Innovations The accuracy of inflation measurement may be improved by technological advancements such as artificial intelligence and data analytics. The collection and analysis of data may be improved, which would give policymakers and investors with more nuanced insights into the dynamics of inflation.

Strategies that are resilient to inflation and support sustainable investing:

There are new factors that investors need to take into consideration as the focus on sustainable investing continues to rise. Companies that are able to demonstrate resilience to environmental, social, and governance (ESG) concerns may also be better positioned to negotiate inflationary issues, which has contributed to the development of methods that are resilient to inflation.

The effect that inflation has on savings and investments is a dynamic and diverse component of the economic landscape for the United States. In order for individuals, organizations, and policymakers to successfully negotiate the obstacles that are provided by fluctuating price levels, it is vital to have a comprehensive awareness of the intricacies of inflation and to adopt tactics that are informed.

The erosion of purchasing power is something that savers need to be aware of, and they should look for investment vehicles that deliver meaningful returns for their money, particularly during times of rising inflation. The effects of inflation on an investor's portfolio can be mitigated by the use of methods such as diversification, inflation-protected securities, allocations to inflation-resilient sectors and real assets, and allocations to real assets.

When it comes to setting the economic climate and managing inflationary pressures, central banks and policymakers play a crucial role. The ability to adjust investment plans to changing conditions and to keep aware about inflationary risks is still extremely important in this day and age, which is characterized by globalization, technological breakthroughs, and the ever-changing dynamics of the economy.

The dynamic relationship that exists between inflation, savings, and investments highlights the significance of adopting a financial planning strategy that is both well-informed and highly dynamic. In the face of inflation's ever-present influence, individuals and investors alike are required to maintain vigilance, adapt to developing trends, and make decisions that are in line with their financial goals. This is because economic landscapes are constantly shifting.

Chapter 6

Societal Ramifications

Societal dynamics are built on the foundation of the interdependence of economic, social, and environmental elements. These forces shape the fabric of communities, nations, and the world as a whole. Within the scope of this article, the multifarious ramifications that emerge at the junction of these dimensions are investigated. The essay also investigates the deep relationships that exist between these dimensions and the implications that they have for individuals, institutions, and policymakers. In order to cultivate communities that are sustainable, egalitarian, and resilient, it is vital to have a solid awareness of the societal ramifications. These ramifications include the economic impacts of social disparities as well as the environmental consequences of economic activity.

Inequalities in terms of both employment and social standing:

Income Inequality and Social Mobility: Disparities in the economy, particularly income inequality, can have significant repercussions for society. Persistent disparities in the distribution of income and wealth can be a barrier to social mobility, which in turn reduces the number of prospects for economic advancement. Poverty and unequal access to education and resources are two factors that contribute to the perpetuation of social inequalities, which in turn has an effect on the well-being of both individuals and communities.

Unemployment and Social Strain: Both declining economies and increasing unemployment rates are factors that contribute to the strain that is placed on society. When an individual loses their work, they may feel increased stress, difficulties with their mental health, and strained relationships with their family members. Addressing the issue of unemployment and promoting economic growth that is inclusive are both essential steps in reducing the social repercussions that are associated with economic instability.

Access to Healthcare and Educational Opportunities The state of the economy has an effect on the availability of critical services, such as healthcare and education. It is possible that people with lower incomes would face obstacles in their access to quality healthcare and educational opportunities, which will exacerbate existing health inequities and restrict their ability to move up in the social hierarchy. When it comes to constructing a society that is more equitable, policies that strive to improve access to these services are essential components.

Environmental Degradation and Its Effects on Society:

Vulnerable Communities and Climate Change: The environmental repercussions of human activities, such as climate change, have a disproportionately negative impact on communities who are already vulnerable. It is common for persons with low incomes to reside in regions that are prone to environmental deterioration. These regions are especially susceptible to the negative effects of extreme weather events, increasing sea levels, and pollution in the air and water. Considerations pertaining to climate justice bring to light the significance of tackling environmental problems with a concentration on principles of equity.

Biodiversity and Cultural Heritage Loss of biodiversity, which is caused by the destruction of habitats and the excessive use of natural resources, not only has an effect on ecosystems but also poses a threat to cultural heritage. Native American tribes, who are frequently intimately related to the natural world, are confronted with difficulties as ecosystems deteriorate, causing disruptions to traditional ways of life and diminishing cultural diversity.

Movements for Environmental Justice Environmental justice movements are movements that fight for the equitable distribution of environmental benefits and costs. These movements emphasize the right of all individuals, regardless of their socioeconomic standing, to live in an environment that is healthy. Building societies that are both socially equitable and environmentally sustainable requires a number of critical components, including the recognition and resolution of environmental injustices.

Homogenization of Cultures and the Effects of Globalization:

The economic aspect of globalization has an effect on cultural dynamics, which can result in both enrichment and problems. This is the cultural impact of globalization. In spite of the fact that globalization makes it easier for people to share ideas and engage in cultural exchange, it also raises concerns about the uniformity of cultures. The prevalence of particular cultural narratives and the propagation of values that are targeted toward consumers can have an effect on the traditions and identities of local communities.

The digital revolution, which is a primary driver of economic globalization, has revolutionized social relationships and connection. This is a direct result of the digital revolution. Despite the fact that digital technologies make communication and access to information easier, they also raise concerns over privacy, the digital divide, and the possibility of social isolation. For the purpose of promoting inclusive communities, it is essential to strike a balance between the advantages and disadvantages of digitalization.

The Impact of Technological Developments on Employment Dynamics:

Automation, job displacement, and reskilling are all examples of how technological breakthroughs, particularly in the areas of artificial intelligence and automation, are reshaping the dynamics of employment. There is a correlation between technological breakthroughs and job displacement, despite the fact that they increase productivity. One of the societal repercussions is the requirement for programs that provide retraining and uptraining in order to guarantee that persons are able to adjust to the ever-changing demands of the labor market.

Inequality and the Digital Divide The digitalization of economies has given rise to worries over the digital divide, which refers to the difference that exists between those who have access to digital technology and others who fail to have such access. By preventing individuals from fully participating in the digital economy, socioeconomic gaps in access to the internet and digital skills can perpetuate inequality and make it more difficult for individuals to participate.

Migration Patterns and the Integration of Social Groups:

Economic Migration and Cultural Diversity: Migration patterns are driven by economic inequities and geopolitical problems, which ultimately results in societies that are diverse and multicultural. Despite the fact that economic migration is a contributor to cultural diversity, it also presents obstacles in terms of social integration, inclusion, and the protection of the rights of migrants. The ways in which societies react to migration are a significant factor in the formation of communities that are cohesive and harmonious.

The phenomenon known as "brain drain," in which highly skilled individuals leave their home nations in search of greater economic opportunities, can have repercussions for the development of the countries from which they originated. It is possible that the loss of talented professionals could impede economic progress and make social and economic difficulties in the regions that are left behind even more severe.

Public Health and the Resilience of Societies:

Public health emergencies, such as pandemics, highlight the significance of societal resilience. Pandemics also have the potential to strengthen social cohesion. The economic repercussions of situations involving health emergencies can result in the loss of jobs, instability in the economy, and hardship on society. In order to keep social cohesion intact during times of public health emergencies, it is essential to have robust healthcare systems, social safety nets, and effective communication procedures.

Health Disparities and Access to Healthcare: Access to healthcare is impacted by economic considerations, which in turn leads to health disparities.

It is possible that people with lower means could face obstacles when attempting to get medical care, which will contribute to disparities in health outcomes. It is necessary to have a holistic approach that takes into account both the economic and social factors that influence health in order to properly address these discrepancies.

Social Innovation and Economic Development:

Entrepreneurship and Community Development: Both social innovation and entrepreneurship play an important part in the process of community development and economic empowerment. In order to contribute to inclusive economic development, initiatives that address social concerns, promote sustainable livelihoods, and empower populations who are marginalized are essential constituents.

Corporate social responsibility (CSR) refers to the fact that the role of corporations extends beyond the realm of economic operations to include duties in the areas of social and environmental governance. The implementation of Corporate Social Responsibility (CSR) programs that prioritize social and environmental effect in addition to financial success contributes to the development of a corporate ecosystem that is more sustainable and socially responsible.

Education and the Development of Competencies:

Education is a significant driver of economic and social mobility, and earning a degree is one of the most important factors in determining economic opportunities. People who have completed higher levels of education typically have access to better economic prospects, which contributes to the well-being of that individual as well as the well-being of society. The development of inclusive societies requires the implementation of policies that encourage equal access to educational opportunities of a high standard.

Continuous Education and Adaptability: The ever-changing character of the contemporary economy highlights the significance of continuous education throughout one's entire life. People need to be able to adjust to the ever-evolving technologies and the ever-shifting requirements of the labor market. It is possible to strengthen the resilience of a society in the face of economic shifts by making investments in ongoing educational opportunities and the development of skilled workers.

Policies established by the government and social welfare:

Poverty Alleviation and Social Safety Nets: The policies of the government, especially social safety nets, play a significant role in alleviating the negative effects that economic issues have on society.

Social welfare programs that are well-designed contribute to the alleviation of poverty, the reduction of inequality, and the enhancement of societal resilience in the face of economic uncertainty.

In the context of social equity, regulatory frameworks have the ability to modify economic activity and have an impact on the results of social interactions. There is a correlation between policies that prioritize social equality, environmental sustainability, and fair labor standards with the development of an economic system that is more equitable and inclusive.

Crisis Management and the Development of Societies That Are Resilient:

Preparedness for Pandemics and Economic Stability: The COVID-19 pandemic brought to light the role that crisis preparedness and resilience play in ensuring economic stability. A comprehensive approach that addresses economic vulnerabilities, improves healthcare systems, and maintains social safety nets to help individuals and communities during times of crisis is required in order to construct societies that are resilient.

Environmental Sustainability and Economic Planning: It is necessary for the long-term well-being of society to incorporate environmental sustainability into economic planning procedures. It is possible to contribute to both economic growth and environmental preservation by enacting policies that encourage sustainable development, renewable energy, and responsible resource management.

Obstacles Affecting the Process of Navigating Societal Complications:

Regarding the interrelated nature of difficulties, it is necessary to address the interwoven nature of economic, social, and environmental challenges in order to successfully navigate the implications that society will experience. In the event that these components are compartmentalized, it is possible that the holistic dynamics that shape communities and nations will not be captured.

Concerns Regarding the Short-Term vs the Long-Term:

There are obstacles for policymakers to overcome when trying to strike a balance between short-term economic demands and long-term sustainability aims. Careful analysis is required in order to come up with a solution that strikes the correct balance between the current economic necessities and the goal of developing societies that are resilient and inclusive.

Questions Regarding the Future:

Ethical questions about the impact that technology has on society are becoming increasingly important as technological advancements continue to push the boundaries of what is considered acceptable. In order to shape a future that is both technologically sophisticated and socially responsible, it will be essential to successfully strike a balance between innovation, ethical considerations, concerns about privacy, and the possibility of social disruption.

Global Collaboration and Sustainable Development: In order to address global concerns, such as climate change and economic inequality, it is necessary to engage in joint activities on a worldwide scale. In order to construct a future that is both sustainable and equitable, it is necessary to engage in international collaboration, to share resources, and to make a commitment to tackling the underlying causes of socioeconomic problems.

Resulting from the complex interaction of economic, social, and environmental dynamics, societal consequences are produced. For the purpose of establishing comprehensive strategies that enhance resilience, inclusivity, and sustainability, it is vital to acknowledge the linked nature of these dimensions. In order to successfully manage complex difficulties, communities need to examine them from a holistic viewpoint. This includes resolving economic imbalances and embracing technology breakthroughs while taking ethical considerations into account.

The urgency rests in the cultivation of a balance that prioritizes the well-being of both people and the earth as individuals, institutions, and policymakers jointly engage in the process of building the future. It is possible for societies to construct robust foundations that are able to resist difficulties and pave the way for a future that is more just, inclusive, and sustainable if they embrace social innovation, equitable economic development, and environmental sustainability.

6.1 Hyperinflation's Social and Economic Toll

An excessive and rapid increase in the overall price level of products and services is referred to as hyperinflation. This phenomenon is a serious economic issue that can have significant repercussions for society. This essay investigates the complex dynamics of hyperinflation and the dual influence that it has on the economic systems as well as the social fabric of communities. Individuals, communities, and nations are left with permanent scars as a result of hyperinflation, which includes the depreciation of purchasing power and social unrest. This highlights the critical need for sound economic management and crisis mitigation techniques.

Hyperinflation is defined as follows:

Characteristics and Limits: Hyperinflation is often defined by inflation rates that are greater than fifty percent per month, which frequently leads to a loss of confidence in the national currency.

The current context of severe inflation causes disruptions to the usual transactions that take place in the economy, reduces savings, and presents considerable hurdles to both people and enterprises.

Causes of Hyperinflation Hyperinflation can be caused by a number of different circumstances, such as an excessive expansion in the money supply, fiscal mismanagement, and a loss of confidence in the currency. The activities of the government, such as the excessive printing of money or the misuse of financial resources, have the potential to set off a self-reinforcing cycle, which further exacerbates inflationary pressures.

The economic impact of hyperinflation is as follows:

There is a quick decline in purchasing power, which is one of the most immediate and severe repercussions of hyperinflation. This is one of the most significant consequences of hyperinflation. As prices continue to rise, the real value of money decreases, leaving individuals with a limited capacity to afford essential products and services. This deterioration has a disproportionately negative impact on individuals who have limited access to financial resources or who have established salaries.

Hyperinflation causes disruptions in the typical economic transactions that take place, making it difficult for businesses to establish pricing, plan investments, and run their operations in a profitable manner. It is possible for there to be a decrease in economic activity as a result of uncertainty regarding future prices and the stability of the currency. This is because businesses and consumers may be reluctant to engage in transactions.

Inequalities in Social Status and the Redistribution of Wealth Hyperinflation frequently leads to a major redistribution of wealth. Others who are able to protect themselves from the effects of inflation by investing in assets such as investments in real estate, foreign currency, or precious metals may fare better than others who are dependent on fixed incomes or cash holdings, who are likely to experience significant economic difficulties. Consequently, this makes socioeconomic inequalities worse and further widens the gaps that already exist within society.

The social toll of hyperinflation is as follows:

Hyperinflation has a significant impact on the level of life of the general people since it brings about a significant reduction in the standard of living. As a result of the prohibitive cost of vital products and services, the overall well-being of the population begins to undergo a deterioration. There is a possibility that a sizable section of the population may be unable to obtain fundamental essentials like basic necessities like food, housing, and healthcare.

Unemployment and the Loss of Livelihoods: The economic turbulence that is linked with hyperinflation frequently results in numerous individuals losing their jobs and their means of subsistence. Businesses, particularly smaller businesses, may have difficulty operating or may even close their doors, which contributes to an increase in the number of people without jobs. For individuals and families, the possibility of financial collapse is a factor that exacerbates the social issues.

Social Unrest and Political Instability: There is a correlation between hyperinflation and social unrest as well as political instability. Protests, demonstrations, and even political upheavals may occur when people are confronted with severe economic difficulties and think that there is a lack of competent governance from their government. The loss of public faith in institutions can have repercussions for the cohesiveness of society that can continue for indefinite periods of time.

In the past, there have been instances of hyperinflation

The hyperinflation that occurred during the Weimar Republic in Germany, which lasted from 1921 to 1923, is considered to be among the most infamous in the history of the world. The economic consequences of World War I and excessive money production were the primary factors that contributed to the skyrocketing of prices to astronomical proportions. As a result of the value of the German mark plummeting, citizens were forced to contend with poor economic situations, which led to social turmoil.

The hyperinflation that Zimbabwe experienced in the early 2000s is yet another striking example. These years span from 2000 to 2009. Both hyperinflation and a decline in agricultural production were caused by political and economic incompetence, which included controversial land changes but also contributed to the collapse. People in Zimbabwe were confronted with significant economic difficulties, and the value of the Zimbabwean currency was fast declining.

Responses from the Government and the Implications for Policy:

Currency Reforms: When confronted with hyperinflation, governments may choose to implement currency reforms, such as redenomination or the introduction of a new currency. While the purpose of these steps is to restore trust, it is important to note that they do not address the fundamental economic concerns that are driving hyperinflation and may only bring short respite.

Support from International Organizations and Stabilization of the Economy Governments that are struggling with hyperinflation may request support from international organizations such as the International Monetary Fund (IMF) or the World Bank.

For the purpose of addressing the underlying factors that contribute to hyperinflation, it is possible to adopt economic stabilization programs. These programs may include legislative reforms, fiscal discipline, and structural improvements.

Problems Associated with the Management of Hyperinflation:

Once hyperinflation has taken hold, it is difficult to regain faith in monetary policy. This is because of the credibility of monetary policy. In order to reestablish confidence in the eyes of the general public and international investors, governments need to demonstrate that they are committed to adhering to good economic principles, transparent governance, and cautious fiscal management.

Social Safety Nets: The social toll that hyperinflation exacts highlights the significance of having social safety nets that are both efficient and effective. It is imperative that governments make the welfare of vulnerable populations a top priority by providing aid for fundamental necessities, medical care, and educational opportunities. In order to lessen the negative impact on individuals and families, it is possible to construct social safety nets that are resilient.

Future Considerations and Lessons Learned from the Experience:

Management of the Budget: The occurrence of hyperinflation highlights the significance of responsible economic policies and the implementation of careful budgetary management. In order to forestall the emergence of hyperinflationary forces, governments must refrain from printing an excessive amount of money, running budgetary deficits that cannot be sustained, and mismanaging their finances.

Diversification of Economic Activities: Increasing economic resilience can be accomplished by diversifying the economy and decreasing reliance on a particular industry or source of revenue. Countries that are unduly dependent on a particular industry, such as agriculture or natural resources, may be more susceptible to the effects of external shocks that contribute to hyperinflation.

Accountability and Transparent Governance: The rule of law, accountability, and transparency in governance are all key components in the process of preserving public trust and confidence in institutions. Accountability should be a top priority for governments when it comes to economic management. This will ensure that policies are developed and put into effect with the population's best interests in mind.

Collaboration and aid on an International Scale: Hyperinflation frequently necessitates the participation of international partners and aid.

It is possible to contribute to the stabilization of the economy and the alleviation of social hardships by engaging with international organizations, seeking the opinion of experts, and implementing changes in conjunction with the global community.

This harsh reminder of the fragility of economic institutions and the significant impact that hyperinflation has on the lives of individuals is brought about by the social and economic toll that hyperinflation exacts. Hyperinflation creates lasting scars on societies, impacting livelihoods, social cohesion, and political stability. This is in addition to the startling figures and economic indicators that emerge as a result of hyperinflation.

The impacts of hyperinflation can be mitigated by the implementation of a plan that is both comprehensive and coordinated, taking into account both the economic and social components. In order to prevent and effectively manage hyperinflation, it is essential to have prudent fiscal management, transparent governance, and international collaboration within the framework. Understanding the lessons that may be learned from past precedents and putting those lessons into practice in order to construct resilient economic systems can help contribute to a more stable and fair future, protecting society from the destructive effects of hyperinflation.

6.2 Strains on Businesses, Employment, and Social Stability

The complicated relationship that exists between businesses, employment, and social stability is the foundation upon which any society that is thriving is built. There are a number of reasons that can exert strains on these essential components as economic landscapes continue to change. These strains can have an impact not just on the prosperity of enterprises and the availability of employment opportunities, but also on the overall stability of communities. This essay dives into the myriad of issues that businesses, the workforce, and society cohesion are confronted with. It investigates the interwoven nature of these dynamics and proposes solutions to negotiate the strains that are placed on enterprises, employment, and social stability.

Potential Obstacles Facing Businesses:

Uncertainty in the Economy: Businesses function within the larger economic framework, and uncertainty can present substantial problems to the businesses doing business. An unpredictable environment is created when there is economic volatility, swings in consumer demand, and global events such as financial crises or pandemics. This environment can put a strain on business operations, planning, and growth strategies.

Disruptions Caused by Technology Rapid technological breakthroughs have the potential to cause disruptions to traditional business paradigms. Businesses that are unable to adjust to the developments in technology run the risk of becoming irrelevant.

Businesses have both opportunities and challenges as a result of the integration of automation, artificial intelligence, and digitalization, which necessitates continuous innovation and agility on their part.

Internationalization and the Vulnerabilities of Supply Chains: Companies that operate in a worldwide economy are confronted with the difficulties that come with interconnected supply chains. It is possible for disruptions, such as natural catastrophes, geopolitical conflicts, or trade disputes, to have an effect on the availability of inputs, manufacturing processes, and the overall resilience of enterprises that operate on a global scale.

Employment Obstacles and Challenges:

Employment Displacement Caused by Automation Automation and technological breakthroughs have the potential to cause employment displacement in some industries such as the manufacturing sector. It is possible that automation will lessen the demand for certain manual or routine jobs, which will make it more difficult for people in certain industries to shift into new roles. However, automation does increase productivity.

Work in Precarious Situations and the Gig Economy The advent of the gig economy has brought about new dynamics in the employment marketplace. Despite the fact that it gives workers more freedom, it can also result in job insecurity, a lack of employment benefits, and difficulties in ensuring a stable income. A significant factor to take into consideration is how to strike a balance between the advantages of gig labor and the requirement for employment security.

Unemployment and Global Economic Downturns There is a correlation between global economic downturns and widespread unemployment. This is something that can be seen during times of financial crisis. It is possible for businesses that are experiencing financial difficulties to resort to layoffs or downsizing, which only serves to exacerbate unemployment rates and contribute to economic uncertainty.

Considerations Pertaining to Social Stability:

The existence of social disparities is a direct result of economic issues, such as income inequality, which contribute to the existence of social disparities. Disparities in money, education, and access to opportunities can put a strain on social stability by encouraging dissatisfaction and weakening a feeling of justice and social cohesion within communities. This can lead to a strain on social cooperation.

There is a correlation between high levels of young unemployment and social unrest. If youth unemployment is high, it can create social discontent.

There is a possibility that young people who are confronted with restricted employment options could become dissatisfied with the systems of society, which could potentially fuel protests, rallies, or other forms of social instability.

Mental health and overall well-being can be negatively impacted by factors such as unemployment, economic uncertainty, and stress in the workplace. These factors can have a negative impact on mental health. They may suffer increased tension, anxiety, and a sense of insecurity, which can have an influence not just on their own lives but also on the social fabric of communities. Individuals who are experiencing job loss or economic troubles may have these experiences.

Methods to Deal with the Pressures that Businesses Are Under:

Adaptation and Innovation: In order to successfully traverse problems, businesses need to place a priority on both innovation and adaptation. Companies are able to maintain their competitiveness and resilience in the face of economic uncertainty if they embrace technical improvements, investigate new business models, and cultivate a culture of innovation.

The diversification of corporate operations and supply chains can help to improve resilience. Risk management is another important aspect of diversification. Companies that are better positioned to endure disruptions and handle swings in the economic climate are those that rely on a diverse range of revenue streams and have excellent risk management methods.

Incorporating sustainable practices into corporate operations not only coincides with societal and environmental goals, but it also promotes long-term resilience. This is because sustainable practices are considered to be environmentally friendly. Businesses that place a higher priority on environmental, social, and governance (ESG) factors are frequently in a better position to establish trust and stability within the communities they operate out of.

Strategies for Overcoming Obstacles in the Workplace:

Investing in Education and Training Businesses have the ability to make a positive contribution to the stability of employment by investing in training and education programs. The ability of employees to adapt to changing demands in the labor market and to improve their employability in the face of technological advancements is enhanced when training and opportunities to improve skills are made available to them.

Work Arrangements That Are Flexible The adoption of flexible work arrangements, such as the ability to work from home, part-time schedules, and gig work models, can provide a balance between the flexibility and stability of employment.

The implementation of these agreements enables firms to meet a wide range of demands while also offering employees with a variety of alternatives.

Employment Policies That Are Socially Responsible Businesses have the ability to improve social stability by implementing employment policies that are socially responsible. In addition to encouraging employee loyalty and lowering turnover rates, a pleasant work environment is created through the implementation of inclusive hiring policies, fair compensation, and benefits standards.

Methods to Encourage the Maintenance of Social Order:

Engagement with Local Communities and Corporate Social Responsibility (CSR): Engaging with local communities and putting corporate social responsibility (CSR) projects into practice can help to improve societal stability. The establishment of beneficial relationships with stakeholders is facilitated by businesses that make active contributions to the development of communities, provide support for local initiatives, and solve societal concerns.

Inclusion and Diversity Promotion: Embracing diversity and working to create an inclusive environment in the workplace are both factors that contribute to societal stability. Businesses that place a high priority on diversity and inclusion programs are able to build workplaces that are reflective of the larger social fabric, which in turn helps to cultivate a sense of belonging and cohesion within their workforce.

Programmes for Employee Well-Being and Mental Health Programmes:

The implementation of employee well-being initiatives is something that organizations may do in recognition of the influence that stress in the workplace and economic uncertainty have on mental health. It is possible that these programs will include resources for mental health, counseling services, and attempts to encourage a good balance between work and personal life.

Policies and Support Mechanisms Implemented by the Government:

Employment Assistance Programs: Governments play a significant role in providing assistance to businesses and maintaining employment stability through the implementation of specific policies. Increasing the overall economic resilience of the economy can be accomplished through the implementation of employment support programs, training efforts, and job development measures.

The provision of robust social safety nets, which may include unemployment compensation, healthcare coverage, and housing help, serves as a safety net for persons who are experiencing economic difficulties. It is possible for the government to contribute to social stability by addressing the urgent needs of vulnerable groups through the implementation of policies that prioritize social welfare.

International Cooperation and the Most Effective Methods Present: The sharing of best practices is made possible by international collaboration, which enables enterprises, governments, and organizations to share their best practices with one another. Learning from successful techniques that have been adopted in a variety of situations can provide valuable insight that can be used to design effective tactics for navigating problems and promoting stability.

Governance of the Global Economy: Increasing the effectiveness of global economic governance frameworks is a factor that leads to stability. Collaboration between states, international organizations, and institutions makes it easier to coordinate solutions to economic issues. This, in turn, reduces the likelihood of economic downturns on a global scale and ensures a more stable environment for enterprises and employment opportunities.

Economic dynamics are characterized by their complexity and interconnectedness, which is highlighted by the strains placed on enterprises, employment, and social stability. Businesses have a vital role in establishing the employment environment and promoting social stability during the process of navigating problems, adapting to technological developments, and contributing to the well-being of society.

Businesses are able to remain resilient and communities are able to maintain their stability when they implement strategies that prioritize innovation, sustainability, and socially responsible activities. The implementation of policies that encourage employment, eliminate social inequities, and promote general societal cohesiveness requires collaboration between governments, corporations, and international stakeholders.

In order to successfully navigate the demands that are being placed on enterprises, employment, and social stability, it is necessary to take a holistic strategy that takes into consideration the quality of life of individuals, the adaptability of businesses, and the larger social fabric. The ability to construct robust foundations that can endure economic challenges and promote stability in an economic landscape that is always shifting can be achieved by societies through the promotion of innovation, the acceptance of social responsibility, and the implementation of policies that are supportive.

6.3 Public Reaction and Political Ramifications

One of the most important aspects of the intricate web that is responsible for the formation of societies is the public's reaction to significant events and the political repercussions that follow. It is a dynamic process that influences governance, policy decisions, and the overall direction of a nation. This process is influenced by a variety of events, including natural catastrophes and pandemics, political scandals, and economic crises. The public's response and the following impact on political landscapes are all examples of this dynamic process. This essay looks into the complex dynamics of public reaction and its political repercussions, examining the diverse nature of this connection and its significance in the context of modern societal difficulties. Specifically, the essay focuses on the politics of the public reaction.

The Dynamics of Interactions with the Public:

Emotional Reactions to Significant Events Reactions from the general public to significant events are frequently characterized by a variety of emotions, including fear, wrath, sadness, and empathy. When it comes to establishing the collective mindset and driving subsequent behaviors, the emotional responses of individuals and groups play a significant influence in shaping the collective mindset.

Distribution of Information and the Influence of the Media The transmission of information through a variety of media channels has a considerable impact on the way the public perceives and reacts to what is happening. It is impossible to overstate the significance of the media's involvement in shaping narratives, drawing attention to particular aspects of an event, and affecting the emotion of the general population. Coverage in the media has the potential to either calm or escalate public sentiments, depending on how it is used.

Amplification of Voices and Social Media: The introduction of social media has brought about a significant change in the mechanisms that govern public reaction. Individuals are provided with a direct conduit via which they can voice their opinions, share information, and rally support through the use of platforms such as Twitter, Facebook, and Instagram. There is the potential for social media to magnify voices, make it easier for groups to take action, and contribute to the quick dissemination of information.

Various Categories of Critical Events and the Reactions of the Public:

Natural Disasters and Humanitarian Crises: The public's responses to natural disasters and humanitarian crises are frequently characterized by a strong desire to assist and support the communities that have been touched by these events. People who are trying to meet the immediate needs of individuals who have been affected frequently respond by making donations, volunteering their time, and making requests for foreign assistance.

Responses of the Public to Health Emergencies and Pandemics The responses of the general public to health emergencies, such as pandemics, vary depending on factors such as the perceived severity of the situation, the response of the government, and personal experiences. There is a widespread prevalence of fear, misinformation, and demands for decisive action from the government. Additionally, there are those who may engage in solidarity actions and community support.

Political Scandals and Governance concerns: Political scandals and concerns connected to governance frequently provoke significant emotions from the general population. Indignation, demonstrations, and calls for accountability are the characteristics that define these responses. The dissatisfaction of the general public can result in fluctuations in political power, calls for institutional reforms, and increased participation in civic life.

Crisis in the Economy and Rising Unemployment Rates: Both economic downturns and rising unemployment rates cause public concern and discontent. It is possible for individuals and communities to react by making demands for economic assistance, undertaking initiatives to create jobs, and scrutinizing the economic policies of the government. Unrest and demonstrations in society can be the outcome of what people perceive to be economic inequalities.

The Social and Political Consequences of the Public Reaction:

Alterations in Public Opinion and Trust in Institutions The reactions of the general public to very significant events have the potential to bring about alterations in public opinion and trust in institutions. The public's trust can be maintained or restored by effective crisis management and clear communication. On the other hand, perceived failures can undermine confidence and impact the outcomes of elections.

Elections and Political Transitions: The political repercussions of popular reaction is frequently represented in electoral processes. Electoral procedures are also a source of political transition. Voters have the ability to hold incumbents accountable for their responses to significant events, which can result in changes in political leadership, alterations in the dynamics of parties, and the formation of new political movements for political change.

Changes in Policy and Legislative Responses: The responses of the public on policy decisions and legislative responses are influenced by public reactions. Governments have the ability to adopt reforms based on popular requests, as well as emergency measures, commit resources to address specific problems, and implement emergency measures. It is necessary to have a nuanced grasp of public mood in order to develop policies that are in line with the requirements and anticipations of the population in order to have effective government.

Strong reactions from the general population have the potential to be a catalyst for social movements and activity. It is common for movements for social justice, environmental protection, or political reform to develop momentum in response to significant occurrences. By reshaping political agendas, influencing governmental priorities, and contributing to long-term societal change, these movements have the potential to impact societies.

The Management of Emergencies and Communication in the Government:

Transparent Communication: It is vital for the government to effectively communicate during critical events in order to effectively manage these reactions from the public. The establishment of trust and the reduction of the likelihood of panic or disinformation are both facilitated by the government's commitment to transparency, the broadcast of factual information, and the clear articulation of its actions.

Strategies for Crisis Management It is imperative that governments put into action effective crisis management strategies that give priority to both the immediate needs of the public and the long-term resolution of the problem. A good crisis management strategy includes taking preventative actions, demonstrating empathy, and making a commitment to addressing the concerns of the public.

Engagement and Participation of the Civil Public:

Participation of Communities and Recognition of Local efforts: Increasing public participation can be accomplished by involving communities in decision-making processes and by recognizing local efforts. A sense of ownership and collective responsibility can be fostered by governments that actively seek the input of a wide variety of communities and incorporate the viewpoints of local residents into the decision-making process about policy.

Education and Information Campaigns: The amount of understanding and awareness of the general public is a significant factor in determining how they react. For the purpose of ensuring that the general public is provided with reliable information regarding important events, governments ought to make investments in education and information initiatives. Citizens who are well-informed are in a better position to make a good contribution to the responses of society.

Striking a Balance Between Political Reality and Public Opinion:

Regarding political responsiveness, governments are required to take into account broader political realities while also being attentive to the sentiments of the general population. It is necessary to take a nuanced approach that takes into account the reactions of the public without compromising the ability to make strategic decisions in order to strike a balance between the need to address urgent concerns and the long-term aims of the government.

Constructing Resilience in Governance In order to construct resilience in governance, it is necessary to strengthen institutions, cultivate a culture of adaptation, and anticipate possible difficulties. When it comes to navigating public reactions, adapting to changing circumstances, and maintaining stability, governments that value resilience are better positioned.

There is a dynamic interplay that defines the trajectory of societies, and it is represented by public reaction and the political repercussions of that reaction. Understanding and responding to the sentiments of the public is essential for efficient administration. This is true for everything from the grassroots activism that drives social change to the electoral repercussions that determine political leadership.

The ability of governments to handle public emotions is becoming increasingly important as societies struggle to cope with a wide range of critical events, ranging from health crises to environmental issues. When combined with strategic crisis management, an approach that is both responsive and transparent has the potential to contribute to the development of trust, the promotion of resilience, and eventually the guarantee that the political repercussions of public reactions will directly result in positive outcomes for society. In order to build a political environment that is more robust and responsive in the face of a world that is always changing, it is necessary to acknowledge the potential of collective action, informed decision-making, and inclusive government.

Chapter 7

Navigating the Future

The future is a complex web of unpredictability, difficulties, and possibilities all woven together seamlessly. A proactive and forward-thinking strategy is required in order to successfully navigate the intricacies of a world that is always changing. In this paper, we investigate the various approaches that can be taken to construct resilient societies that are able to adjust to new circumstances, flourish, and make a good contribution to the overall landscape of the world. Every aspect, from technical developments to environmental sustainability, economic resilience, and social equality, plays a significant part in determining the course that our collective future will take.

Some Recent Developments in Technology:

Technology that is both innovative and ethical: embracing technology breakthroughs is of the utmost importance when it comes to navigating the future. Technological advancements in fields such as artificial intelligence, biotechnology, and renewable energy have the potential to provide solutions to urgent problems that are affecting the entire world. In spite of this, ethical concerns ought to be the driving force behind technological growth in order to guarantee that breakthroughs are in accordance with society values and put the welfare of mankind top priority.

Training and education: In order to successfully navigate a future that will be influenced by technology, it is vital to have a workforce that is both skilled and adaptable. The preparation of individuals for the ever-changing labor markets can be accomplished by investing in education that cultivates critical thinking, creativity, and digital literacy. Initiatives for lifelong learning and programs for upskilling contribute to the development of a workforce that is able to capitalize on the advantages brought about by technological advancement.

Digital Inclusion and Accessibility: In order to construct a future that is inclusive, it is essential to bridge the digital divide. The promotion of equal opportunities and the prevention of the worsening of existing disparities can be accomplished by ensuring that all segments of society have access to digital technology and are literate. Collaboration between governments, corporations, and international organizations is required in order to develop policies that give digital inclusion a higher priority.

Sustainability of the Environment:

Action on Climate Change and Renewable Energy: The future is dependent on finding a solution to the increasingly urgent problem of climate change. It is imperative that governments, corporations, and individuals all make a commitment to achieving aggressive climate action targets, that they migrate to renewable energy sources, and that they apply sustainable practices. The effective mitigation of the effects of climate change on a global scale requires the participation of international partners.

Conservation of Biodiversity and Restoration of Ecosystems: Both the preservation of biodiversity and the restoration of ecosystems are essential elements of a future that is sustainable. A significant contribution to the maintenance of the natural equilibrium of the globe is made by conservation efforts, reforestation projects, and sustainable land management measures. One of the most important things for the long-term health of the environment is to acknowledge the interdependence of ecosystems.

Circular Economy and Sustainable Practices: The transition to a circular economy, in which resources are reused, recycled, and repurposed, is essential for the development of sustainable practices. A future in which economic growth and environmental preservation are in harmony can be achieved by the adoption of environmentally friendly business practices, the reduction of waste, and the prioritization of sustainable supply chains by businesses.

Economic Resilience:

Innovation and Diversification: In order to construct economic resilience, it is necessary to integrate both innovation and diversification. During times of economic instability, countries that are highly reliant on particular industries are susceptible to vulnerability. Investments in research and development, the encouragement of entrepreneurial endeavors, and the diversification of economic activity all contribute to the creation of resilient and adaptive economies.

Global Cooperation and Trade Policies: In a world that is more interconnected, global cooperation is something that is absolutely necessary for maintaining economic stability. It is imperative that nations engage in fair trade practices, create agreements that are beneficial to both parties, and work together to overcome the issues that the global economy faces. The impact of economic crises can be lessened through international collaboration, which also serves to develop a global economy that is more linked and robust.

There should be social safety nets and inclusive policies in place, and the well-being of all residents should be the first priority for economic resilience. The establishment of social safety nets, which may include comprehensive healthcare systems, unemployment compensation, and access to educational opportunities, functions as a basis for inclusive economic growth.

For the purpose of ensuring that economic success is distributed evenly throughout society, governments are obligated to enact policies that aim to eliminate income disparity.

Social Equity:

Participation and Governance That Are Inclusive The development of resilient societies requires the implementation of inclusive governance processes. During the decision-making process, governments ought to make a concerted effort to solicit the participation of a wide range of views. The cohesion and resilience of a society can be improved by the implementation of inclusive policies that seek to eliminate socioeconomic inequalities, advance equal opportunities, and protect human rights.

Both access to education and healthcare are essential components of social fairness. Education and healthcare are vital cornerstones. The establishment of a foundation for individual and societal well-being can be accomplished by ensuring that all citizens have access to high-quality education and healthcare. The implementation of policies that give priority to these areas will lead to a future in which every person will have the opportunity to realize their ultimate potential.

Diversity of culture and inclusiveness: Societies that are resilient appreciate and accept the diversity of their cultural backgrounds. Social cohesiveness can be improved by the implementation of policies that encourage inclusiveness, tolerance, and understanding. The appreciation of cultural diversity is beneficial to the development of creativity, the promotion of a sense of belonging, and the consolidation of the social fabric of communities.

Crisis Management and the Development of Societies That Are Resilient:

Pandemic Preparedness and Economic Stability: Recent occurrences on a global scale have brought to light the significance of being well-prepared for any kind of emergency. A comprehensive approach that addresses economic vulnerabilities, improves healthcare systems, and ensures social safety nets to support individuals and communities during times of crisis is required in order to build societies that are resilient.

Environmental Sustainability and Economic Planning: It is necessary for the long-term well-being of society to incorporate environmental sustainability into economic planning procedures. It is possible to contribute to both economic growth and environmental preservation by enacting policies that encourage sustainable development, renewable energy, and responsible resource management.

Obstacles to Overcome When Navigating the Societal Ramifications:

Regarding the interrelated nature of difficulties, it is necessary to address the interwoven nature of economic, social, and environmental challenges in order to successfully navigate the implications that society will experience. In the event that these components are compartmentalized, it is possible that the holistic dynamics that shape communities and nations will not be captured.

Concerns Regarding the Short-Term vs the Long-Term:

There are obstacles for policymakers to overcome when trying to strike a balance between short-term economic demands and long-term sustainability aims. Careful analysis is required in order to come up with a solution that strikes the correct balance between the current economic necessities and the goal of developing societies that are resilient and inclusive.

Considerations for the Future:

Ethical questions about the impact that technology has on society are becoming increasingly important as technological advancements continue to push the boundaries of what is considered acceptable. In order to shape a future that is both technologically sophisticated and socially responsible, it will be essential to successfully strike a balance between innovation, ethical considerations, concerns about privacy, and the possibility of social disruption.

Global Collaboration and Sustainable Development: In order to address global concerns, such as climate change and economic inequality, it is necessary to engage in joint activities on a worldwide scale. In order to construct a future that is both sustainable and equitable, it is necessary to engage in international collaboration, to share resources, and to make a commitment to tackling the underlying causes of socioeconomic problems.

An approach that is both all-encompassing and forward-thinking is necessary in order to successfully navigate the future, which is a community undertaking. Creating resilient societies requires a number of different aspects, each of which plays an important part. These aspects include economic resilience, social equality, and environmental sustainability, as well as technology innovation. In order to create a future in which individuals, communities, and nations are able to adapt, grow, and positively contribute to the world, it is important to draw lessons from successful models, solve interlinked concerns, and prioritize inclusive governance.

At a time when we are at a crossroads in a world that is undergoing fast change, it is of the utmost importance that we cultivate a balance that places equal importance on the overall health and happiness of both people and the earth.

It is possible for society to develop the resilience necessary to handle the uncertainties and complexities of the future by embracing social innovation, equitable economic development, and environmental sustainability. This will ensure a route toward a world that is more sustainable, inclusive, and affluent.

7.1 Implementing Sustainable Economic Policies

During this time when governments are struggling to deal with the issues of climate change, social injustice, and environmental degradation, sustainable economic policies are at the forefront of talks taking place all over the world. It is becoming more and more obvious that it is essential to strike a balance between economic growth, environmental stewardship, and social equality. An examination of the ideas and techniques that underpin the implementation of sustainable economic policies is presented in this essay. The focus is on the ways in which nations may support resilient and equitable development while simultaneously protecting the planet for future generations.

The Foundations of Economic Policies, Which Are Sustainable:

Triple Bottom Line Approach: The triple bottom line approach is the foundation of sustainable economic strategies. This method places an emphasis on the interconnected goals of economic growth, environmental stewardship, and social equity. In order to achieve a harmonic and balanced approach to growth, policies that take into consideration all three dimensions simultaneously endeavor to achieve this goal.

Long-Term Planning and Vision: In order to sustainably implement economic policies, it is necessary to have a long-term vision that extends beyond the political cycles. The planning process for resilience and sustainability entails the establishment of distinct goals, the anticipation of obstacles, and the formulation of policies that encourage long-term economic growth while simultaneously limiting adverse effects on the environment and society.

Integration of Environmental and Social factors: In order to take a comprehensive approach to sustainability, it is necessary to incorporate environmental and social factors into the process of making economic decisions. In order to guarantee inclusive growth, policies need to take into account the environmental footprint that economic activities leave behind, encourage conservation, and attempt to solve socio economic inequities.

The core principles of economically sustainable policies are as follows:

Green Growth and the Circular Economy: Green growth places an emphasis on economically viable development that is both ecologically friendly.

It is possible to reduce the negative influence on the environment while simultaneously fostering economic expansion through the implementation of policies that encourage energy efficiency, renewable energy sources, and a circular economy, which is characterized by the reuse and recycling of resources.

Social fairness is a fundamental component of economically sustainable policies, and inclusive development is a key component of their implementation. In order to foster inclusive growth, it is necessary to make certain that the economic gains are distributed evenly throughout all sectors of society, irrespective of their socioeconomic standing. Policies that prioritize vulnerable people, offer equal access to education and healthcare, and address wealth disparity are all factors that contribute to social fairness.

Environmental Conservation and Biodiversity Protection: Policies that give environmental conservation and biodiversity protection a higher priority are absolutely necessary for the achievement of sustainable development. The preservation of ecosystems and the preservation of the ecological balance of the globe are both promoted by the implementation of measures to avoid deforestation, safeguard natural areas, and limit pollution.

The Instruments for the Implementation of Ecologically Sound Economic Policies:

Taxes on carbon emissions and carbon pricing mechanisms: Carbon pricing mechanisms, such as cap-and-trade systems or carbon taxes, provide businesses with an incentive to limit the amount of carbon emissions they manufacture. Internalizing the environmental cost of economic operations is made possible by these instruments, which encourage businesses to adopt environmentally responsible practices and invest in technology that are cleaner.

It is possible for governments to accelerate the transition to sustainable energy by providing subsidies and incentives for renewable energy sources. This can be accomplished through the provision of subsidies and incentives. The promotion of environmental sustainability, the creation of jobs, and the acceleration of economic growth in the renewable energy industry are all outcomes of providing support for clean energy technologies such as solar, wind, and others.

A significant instrument for promoting responsible business conduct is the establishment of clear regulatory frameworks that demand sustainable practices. These frameworks should be established in order to ensure that sustainable practices are met. Through the implementation of regulations that restrict emissions, encourage waste reduction, and enforce environmental standards, industries are guided toward more ethical and environmentally responsible behavior.

Obstacles to Overcoming When Attempting to Implement Sustainable Economic Policies:

Trade-offs in the Short-Term vs the Long-Term:

In order to implement economically viable policies, it is frequently necessary to navigate short-term trade-offs in order to achieve long-term rewards. The task of persuading stakeholders that the initial expenses of migrating to sustainable practices would yield greater advantages in terms of economic resilience, environmental health, and social well-being is a difficulty that policymakers must navigate.

Cooperation on a worldwide Scale and Harmonization of Regulatory Policies: In order to achieve sustainable economic policies, worldwide cooperation and regulatory harmonization are required. Businesses that are attempting to embrace sustainable practices may face difficulties for a variety of reasons, including differences in environmental rules and labor standards across countries. The promotion of international cooperation and standardization is absolutely necessary in order to achieve a global economy that is more egalitarian and sustainable.

Strategies for Overcoming Obstacles and Other Obstacles:

Public Awareness and Stakeholder Engagement: Increasing public awareness and involving stakeholders are two of the most important tactics for overcoming obstacles in the process of putting sustainable economic policies into effect. It is possible to garner support for policy efforts by educating the general public about the advantages of sustainability. Additionally, engaging with businesses, communities, and advocacy groups can ensure a more inclusive and collaborative approach.

For the success of sustainable economic policies, it is essential to encourage participation from the private sector. This can be accomplished by providing incentives for private sector engagement. Businesses that embrace environmentally responsible practices may be eligible for cash incentives, tax rebates, or access to support from their respective governments. In order to assist bridge the gap between commercial interests and environmental responsibility, it is helpful to create an environment that is favorable to sustainable innovation initiatives.

Building Capacity and Transferring Technology: Initiatives that aim to build capacity and transfer technology are absolutely necessary in order to provide developing countries with the ability to execute economic policies that are sustainable. The capacity of nations to adopt and profit from sustainable practices is improved through international cooperation that helps to expedite the transfer of sustainable technologies and provides assistance for the growth of local capacity.

Prospects for the Further Future and Innovations:

The advancement of technology is the key to unlocking sustainable solutions, and technological innovations are the key to unlocking these solutions. There are potential pathways that can be pursued in order to address environmental concerns while simultaneously supporting economic development. These include innovations in clean energy, sustainable agriculture or waste reduction technologies.

Sustainable food systems and regenerative agriculture: Regenerative agriculture, which focuses on restoring soil health and biodiversity, is gaining ground as a sustainable method to food production. Regenerative agriculture also focuses on achieving sustainable food systems. Policy initiatives that encourage regenerative agriculture and provide support for sustainable food systems are beneficial to both the preservation of the environment and the guaranteeing of food security.

Blockchain Technology and Transparent Supply Chains Blockchain technology offers a method that is both transparent and decentralized for tracking and verifying supply chains. By incorporating blockchain technology into supply chain management, firms can improve their capacity to trace their products, encourage ethical sourcing, and guarantee that they adhere to responsible and sustainable business practices.

The implementation of sustainable economic policies is a multi-faceted enterprise that needs a commitment to striking a balance between economic growth, environmental stewardship, and social equality. The concepts of the triple bottom line approach, the integration of environmental and social factors, and the utilization of mechanisms such as carbon pricing and incentives for renewable energy are some of the ways in which nations can pave the path for development that is both resilient and equitable.

Examples of effective models of sustainable economic policy can be found in case studies, such as those of countries in Scandinavia and Costa Rica. Nevertheless, difficulties continue to exist, such as the requirement for global cooperation and the existence of short-term trade-offs. To overcome these problems, it is necessary to implement tactics such as raising public awareness, providing incentives for engagement from the business sector, and implementing technology transfer programs.

With an eye toward the future, we can see that technical advancements, regenerative agriculture, and blockchain technologies present promising opportunities for the development of environmentally responsible economic policies.

It is possible for nations to provide the groundwork for a future in which economic prosperity, environmental sustainability, and social fairness may live happily by embracing these technologies and fostering international collaboration. This will ensure that future generations will inherit a world that is more resilient and equitable.

7.2 Global Cooperation in Monetary Stewardship

The interdependence of economies throughout the world and the interconnectedness of financial markets highlight the significance of international collaboration in the management of monetary resources. In addition to having far-reaching repercussions that transcend beyond national borders, monetary policies, exchange rate regimes, and financial regulations all have such implications. The requirement of global collaboration in monetary stewardship is investigated in depth in this essay. The challenges, benefits, and viable frameworks for supporting stability and inclusivity in the international financial system are also discussed.

The Multifaceted and Interdependent World of Finance:

Globalization and Financial Integration: The process of globalization has resulted in increased financial integration, which has led to the flow of capital, commerce, and investments that transcend national boundaries. Because the financial markets are interrelated, economic events that occur in one region of the world can have repercussions that are felt in other regions of the world. As a result of this interconnection, a collaborative strategy is required in order to effectively manage monetary policy and maintain financial stability.

The mechanisms that govern currency exchange rates are extremely important in international trade and investment. Currency exchange rates play a vital role in both situations. The selection of exchange rate mechanisms, whether they are fixed, floating, or managed float, has an impact on the capacity of nations to compete with one another and on the flow of money around the world. Efforts that are coordinated in the management of currency rates contribute to the maintenance of stable economic circumstances and make international transactions occur more smoothly.

Obstacles Facing the Administration of Global Monetary Policy:

Divergent national interests: governments frequently implement monetary policies that are based on the specific economic situations and priorities of their own nations. The efforts to coordinate global monetary policy can be made more difficult by the presence of divergent national interests, particularly during times of economic crisis. For the purpose of achieving a balance between the requirements of various economies, diplomatic expertise and a mutual comprehension of the interdependence of financial systems are required.

Influence of Domestic policy on International Markets The influence of domestic monetary policy extends beyond the borders of individual nations worldwide. Changing interest rates, engaging in quantitative easing, or imposing capital controls are all examples of decisions that have the potential to influence exchange rates and have a ripple effect on other economies. In order to effectively control these spillovers and reduce the number of unintended consequences, global cooperation is very necessary.

Conflicts over exchange rates and allegations of currency manipulation can give rise to trade tensions and currency wars. Disputes over exchange rates can also lead to charges of currency manipulation. When conflicts of this nature occur, they disturb the normal functioning of the international financial system, which in turn has an effect on trade balances and contributes to economic uncertainty. When it comes to addressing these tensions and fostering a more stable economic climate on a global scale, international collaboration is very necessary.

The Advantages of International Collaboration in the Management of Monetary Resources:

Financial Stability and Crisis Prevention: The enhanced financial stability that results from global collaboration in monetary stewardship is a direct result of the facilitation of early detection and prevention of financial crises worldwide. Through the sharing of information, the coordination of monetary policies, and the establishment of crisis response mechanisms, collaborative efforts contribute to the development of a more resilient international financial system.

Enhanced Policy Effectiveness: The effectiveness of particular measures is amplified when big economies coordinate their monetary policies with one another. In situations where countries align their policies, whether through adjustments to interest rates or the provision of liquidity, the cumulative effect is higher than the total of the actions taken by each nation individually. The increased efficiency contributes to the financial stability of the entire world.

Facilitating Inclusive Economic Growth Global monetary cooperation has the potential to contribute to inclusive economic growth by tackling systemic difficulties that have a disproportionate impact on poorer economies. Initiatives that support sustainable development goals, reduce income inequality, and promote financial inclusion are more likely to be successful when they are supported by joint efforts on the international scale.

Frameworks for International Monetary Cooperation:
The International Monetary Fund (IMF) is an important institution that plays a role in the coordination of monetary policy on a global scale.

In addition to providing a forum for dialogue and economic monitoring, it also offers financial help to member nations that are experiencing difficulties with their balance of payments. It is possible to improve the International Monetary Fund's role in fostering global monetary stability by reforming and strengthening the organization.

G20 and Multilateral Forums: The Group of Twenty (G20) is an organization that brings together key economies to address topics pertaining to the global economy. The participation of leaders in multilateral forums affords them the opportunity to engage in conversation, as well as to coordinate policies and collectively handle difficulties. In order to facilitate more efficient global monetary cooperation, strengthening these platforms can be of great assistance.

Frameworks for Global Financial Regulation It is vital to establish global financial regulatory frameworks in order to address the risks that are associated with investing across international borders. A more robust international financial architecture can be achieved by the harmonization of regulatory norms, the enhancement of transparency, and the coordination of supervisory operations. These frameworks are shaped in large part by organizations such as the Financial Stability Board (FSB), which plays an important role.

Strengthening Cooperation Across the World's Monetary Community:
Reforming International Institutions The International Monetary Fund (IMF) and the World Bank are two examples of international institutions that could benefit from reforming in order to improve their efficiency in fostering global monetary cooperation. To do this, it may be necessary to change voting shares in order to more accurately reflect the economic contributions of emerging economies and to make certain that these institutions continue to be responsive to the ever-changing dynamics of the global economy.

Improving Data Sharing and Surveillance processes It is essential to have improved data sharing and surveillance processes in order to uncover potential financial risks at an earlier stage. The nations should make a commitment to exchanging economic data in an open and honest manner and to working together to ensure that global economic trends are monitored. The ability to respond in a timely manner to newly emerging difficulties can be facilitated by improved data analytics and monitoring.

In order to achieve successful global monetary cooperation, it is essential to promote inclusive decision-making. This involves ensuring that decision-making procedures are inclusive. It is possible to build a sense of ownership and commitment to collaborative initiatives by acknowledging the various needs and views of all nations, particularly rising economies. When it comes to multinational efforts, inclusive decision-making is beneficial to both their legitimacy and their effectiveness.

Considerations for the Future:

Innovations in Financial Technology and Digital Currencies The proliferation of digital currencies and innovations in financial technology presents global monetary cooperation with opportunities as well as difficult difficulties. For the purpose of addressing regulatory concerns, ensuring financial stability, and capitalizing on the potential benefits of emerging technology, central bank digital currencies (CBDCs) and decentralized finance (DeFi) platforms require international collaboration.

The necessity to address climate change necessitates worldwide collaboration in aligning monetary policies with sustainable development goals. Climate finance and sustainable investments are two strategies that can be utilized to achieve this goal. The promotion of green finance, the incorporation of climate risk considerations into monetary regulation, and the encouragement of sustainable investments all contribute to the development of a global economy that is more environmentally sustainable and resilient.

In order to successfully navigate the problems that come with living in a globalized environment, global cooperation in monetary stewardship is absolutely necessary. For the purpose of ensuring stability, inclusivity, and sustainable economic growth, joint efforts become crucial as governments struggle to deal with different interests, currency conflicts, and the possible impact from domestic monetary policy.

Facilitating conversation and coordination are frameworks such as the International Monetary Fund (IMF), the Group of Twenty (G20), and global financial regulatory authorities. In order to strengthen global monetary cooperation, it is essential to take initiatives such as strengthening these institutions, improving data exchange, and fostering decision-making that is inclusive. As the world continues to face new issues, such as climate finance and digital currencies, continuing collaboration will be required in order to design a resilient and inclusive international financial system that is to the benefit of all nations. The spirit of cooperation continues to be of the utmost importance in the effort to achieve a global economy that is both stable and linked.

7.3 Lessons Learned and Strategies for a Stable Financial Future

The global landscape has been witness to economic upheavals, financial crises, and extraordinary difficulties, all of which have influenced the manner in which individuals, corporations, and nations approach the issue of how to maintain financial stability. The purpose of this essay is to examine the lessons that can be gained from historical financial events and to identify solutions that may be utilized to construct a financially secure future. These lessons serve as guideposts for individuals as well as policymakers, and they cover topics such as the significance of the role of innovation and flexibility, as well as the value of wise financial planning.

The Effects of Financial Crises on the Economy:

The International Financial Crisis of 2008 The worldwide financial markets are interrelated, and the 2008 financial crisis serves as a sharp reminder of this interdependence. The loss of Lehman Brothers, the failure of subprime mortgages, and the subsequent banking crisis all had significant repercussions, which ultimately resulted in a severe recession and widespread economic misery. The lessons that may be learned from this crisis highlight the importance of having solid regulatory frameworks, properly managing risks, and being vigilant when monitoring systemic vulnerabilities.

Insights into the cyclical nature of economies can be gained from historical recessions, such as those that occurred in the 1980s and 1990s. These recessions offer useful insights on the nature of economies. The significance of monetary policy instruments, the relevance of fiscal stimulus, and the importance of correcting structural vulnerabilities in financial systems emerge as a unifying thread from this discussion. Taking these lessons into consideration highlights the importance of governments and central banks implementing counter-cyclical measures in order to reduce the negative effects of economic downturns.

Instructions Regarding Personal Finances:

The pandemic caused by the COVID-19 virus brought to light the importance of having finances set up for unexpected expenses. People were confronted with unanticipated difficulties, such as the loss of their jobs and unanticipated bills. The lessons that were learned highlight how important it is to keep an emergency reserve in order to provide a financial cushion during times of uncertainty.

A high amount of personal debt can make financial stress even worse during times of economic depression. Debt management and financial literacy are two important aspects of this. Literacy in finance and responsible management of debt are both absolutely necessary. Financial well-being over the long term can be improved by developing budgets, gaining an understanding of the ramifications of various types of debt, and making decisions based on accurate information regarding finances.

Methods to Ensure a Secure Financial Future:

A varied investment portfolio is necessary in order to construct a secure financial future. Diversification in investments comes into play here. When it comes to matters of money, the old proverb "don't put all your eggs in one basket" is absolutely correct. There is a reduction in risk and a buffer against the impact of market swings when an investment portfolio is diversified across a number of different asset types.

Planning Your Finances for the Long Term: Planning your finances for the long term is an essential component of stability. It is beneficial for individuals and families to establish distinct monetary objectives, devise strategies for saving money, and make investments for the future. This strategy makes it possible to accumulate wealth over a period of time and makes it possible to achieve certain financial milestones by providing a road map.

Innovation and adaptation in Business: In order to successfully manage the economic uncertainties that exist, businesses need to acknowledge and embrace innovation and adaptation. The ability to adapt one's strategy in reaction to shifting market conditions, make use of technological advancements, and recognize new opportunities is of absolutely critical importance. The necessity of resiliency and forward-thinking initiatives is brought to light by the lessons learned from successful startups and businesses.

Economic Resilience Policies of the Government Policymakers have a crucial role in the process of building economic resilience. The implementation of fiscal policies that are solid, the maintenance of financial stability, and the adoption of counter-cyclical measures during economic downturns are all fundamentally important. The necessity of proactive and coordinated measures to help economic recovery is highlighted by the lessons that may be learned from effective and efficient policy responses.

Technology and the Inclusion of Financial Services:

Fintech and Access to Financial Services: The financial environment has been revolutionized as a result of technological breakthroughs, notably in the field of fintech. Through the lessons learnt, the potential of technology to improve financial inclusion has been brought to light. The expansion of access to financial services is facilitated by the introduction of novel financial products, mobile banking, and digital payment methods, particularly in communities that are not adequately served.

Blockchain technology and the rise of decentralized finance (DeFi) both give prospects for redesigning traditional financial institutions. Blockchain technology is referring to the distributed ledger technology that underpins blockchain. The potential for enhanced efficiency, openness, and inclusion in financial transactions is highlighted by the lessons that may be learned from the decentralized finance area. In order to reduce the likelihood of adverse outcomes, policymakers need to find a middle ground between encouraging innovation and ensuring regulatory control.

Lessons Learned from the Resilience of the Economy:

Keeping a Balance Between Economic Growth and Sustainability The lessons that may be learned from economically resilient nations highlight the significance of maintaining a relationship between economic growth and sustainability.

The promotion of sustainable practices, the prioritization of environmental concerns, and the investment in environmentally friendly technologies all contribute to the long-term economic viability of an organization.

Social Safety Nets and Inclusive Policies: In order to construct economic resilience, it is necessary to design policies that are inclusive and give priority to social safety nets. The importance of addressing income inequality, ensuring access to healthcare, and establishing policies that protect vulnerable populations during times of economic difficulty is brought to light by the lessons learned from countries that have effective social welfare systems.

Developing the Capacity to Withstand Economic Stress:

In order to maintain the resilience of the global economy, it is necessary to engage in crisis response activities that involve international coordination. In order to effectively address global concerns, it is essential to have coordinated efforts, information exchange, and collaborative measures, as demonstrated by the lessons learned during the response to the COVID-19 pandemic.

Trade and Economic Partnerships: The lessons that may be learned from prosperous economic partnerships emphasize the advantages of developing trade policies that are open and collaborative. The development of economic resilience requires the cultivation of constructive trade relationships, the diversification of export markets, and the recognition that economic partnerships should contribute to the prosperity of both parties.

Considerations for the Future:

Practices in the Financial Sector That Are Climate-Resilient The global economy is facing severe threats as a result of climate change. The integration of climate-resilient financial practices, the alignment of investments with sustainability goals, and the development of initiatives to alleviate the economic impact of climate-related catastrophes are all future issues that should be taken into account.

Digital Currencies and the Future of Finance The proliferation of digital currencies, central bank digital currencies (CBDCs), and the development of financial technology all present potential and difficulties for the future of finance. It is necessary for policymakers to negotiate the ramifications of these advances in order to guarantee that financial systems will continue to be secure, inclusive, and robust in the face of technological advancements.

The lessons that may be learnt from successful economic models, personal finance experiences, and historical financial events provide vital insights that can be used to construct a financially secure future. These lessons can be utilized by individuals and policymakers alike in order to navigate the economic uncertainties that are present. These lessons range from the significance of smart financial planning to the role that flexibility and innovation play.

The practice of diversity in investments, long-term financial planning, adaptability in company, and the implementation of good government policies are all strategies that can be utilized to ensure a secure financial future. The use of technology, the promotion of financial inclusion, and the placing of an emphasis on sustainability are all factors that contribute to the development of resilience in the face of shifting economic patterns.

The lessons learned and strategies mentioned in this essay serve as a compass for individuals, corporations, and governments that are attempting to attain economic stability and resilience in an environment that is constantly changing on a global scale. This is because the globe is currently grappling with ongoing issues and preparing for future uncertainty.